Best wishes to my brother and Sister
in Christ
Bob and Shirley Hooker
I have spent many pleasant
hours under your good teaching
"Keep serving God and
Keep the Faith"

Arnold B. Ingram
Jan. 7, 2008

GOD BLESSED AMERICA
NO MORE

ARNOLD B. INGRAM

authorHOUSE®

AuthorHouse™
1663 Liberty Drive, Suite 200
Bloomington, IN 47403
www.authorhouse.com
Phone: 1-800-839-8640

AuthorHouse™ UK Ltd.
500 Avebury Boulevard
Central Milton Keynes, MK9 2BE
www.authorhouse.co.uk
Phone: 08001974150

First published by AuthorHouse 12/11/2007

ISBN: 978-1-4343-2445-0 (sc)
ISBN: 978-1-4343-2444-3 (hc)

Library of Congress Control Number: 2007906661

Printed in the United States of America
Bloomington, Indiana

This book is printed on acid-free paper.

In the spring of 1996, the Lord blessed me with a call to Pastor Ashland Avenue Baptist Church, in Latonia, KY. It was not long before I began to hear of the reputation of Arnold as a dedicated student of the Bible and a man known for his attention to detail.

As I got to know Arnold, wanting to utilize his unique gifts and talents, I asked him to begin a new Wednesday evening class geared toward our Sunday School Teachers. Using the text for the upcoming lesson, Arnold utilized his talents by providing our teachers with insight and background research materials for their upcoming lesson. Soon, the class attracted not only teachers, but others sat in on the class to take advantage of his material.

When Arnold told me of his burning desire and sense of God's calling to write a book about the historical understanding of prophecy, I knew it would be well researched and written. The writer has displayed what may be described as God-given. It gave me great pleasure to help get his manuscript into book form. Thank you Arnold B Ingram. I pray you will read this book with an open mind and heart to God's movement in the world around us.

It is the responsibility of every generation to read the "signs of the times," with the understanding that these are the Last Days. Each current event and passing day requires that we re-examine our world through the eyes of Scripture; not because Scripture has changed, but because we have.

This book will help give you an historical perspective on prophecy, bring to light realities that seem lost in today's world, and most importantly it will challenge your way of thinking.

Rev. William C. Class, D. Min.

Arnold has finally written this timely piece of prophetic insight. Over the past 30 years, this topic has been discussed over many meals and /or social occasions. It comes from countless years of study, prayer, and research to find it's way into print.

Arnold is a man of integrity, dedication and humility who writes from a heart filled with understanding and compassion for God and His people. His desire is to share this knowledge and warning with believers and seekers alike. His goal is to help everyone understand this complex history, and how in His infinite wisdom, God warns us that though history, the punishment for sin and rejection of Him is predictable and promised for the future. This book is about the blessings God has for His followers and warnings for His believers about hard times ahead as a consequence of our individual and national sins.

This work is profound but understandable. It is complex, but able to be followed through its passage of time and cast of characters. My prayer is that it will have a profound impact on your understanding of God's Word and His works, and you will experience God's blessings and direction in your future.

Rev. Thomas C. Noyes, PhD

TABLE OF CONTENTS

DECICATION

This Book is fondly dedicated to my dear wife Hazel, my only daughter Kathy, and my three sons Jeff, Mark, and Paul. And to all who love the Lord and cherish His Word, may you be blessed as I have been in life, family, and most of all the Saving Grace of our Lord.

ACKNOWLEDGMENTS

For many years, I have been interested in this subject. As God presented opportunity, I have had several opportunities to teach about God's promises being revealed in the world around us. Several years ago, I began to think about writing a book on the subject, but only recently did I feel the burning desire of God's calling to actually undertake the endeavor.

Over the years, I have read a number of authors who touched on the subject of the Birthright and Scepter Lines of God's promised blessings. Fully understanding that we do not learn in a vacuum, I am well aware that my thoughts and ideas have been influenced by others. While the works listed here have not been directly quoted or referred to in this book, I want to acknowledge some of the writers whose works have been valuable to me. Certainly, this is not an exhaustive list. However, if you want to pursue additional readings on the subject, these are good places in which to start.

Allen, J. H. (1902) **Judah's Scepter and Joseph's Birthright**. Nineteenth Edition, [Electronic Version}

Glover, F.R.A. (1861) **England, the Remnant of Judah, and the Israel of Ephraim**, [Electronic Version].

Grimaldi, A. B. (1885) **The Queen's royal descent from King David the Psalmist.** [Electronic Version} (Pamphlet published by Grimaldi, incorporated in numerous books.)

Tullidge, E. K. (1881) **Ancient Prophecies and Modern Fulfillments**. [Electronic Version]

Wilson, J. (1840) **Our Israelite Origin**: Lectures on Ancient Israel and the Israelinteish Origin of the Modern Nations of Europe. [Electronic Version]

Additionally, the King James Version of Scripture is used within this book unless otherwise stated. There is a great deal of Scripture text in the book in an attempt to make it easier for the reader to follow the train of thought without taking time to look up each passage. I hope you find this useful.

You will quickly notice two things. First, these are all found in "Electronic Media" form. I do thank God for the ease and availability of such rare works over the Internet. Second, these are all older works. The reason for this is that most of the newer authors I have read end up referring back to these works. Additionally, they were written at a time when the research in this field was strong. Today, we are seeing somewhat of a revival of their work as well as new work being done.

Just as I have not learned in a vacuum, neither did this book come into fruition without the help of others. As all writers know, without the help and support of a loving spouse, many books would go unwritten and many bookshelves full of only dust. My wife Hazel is a loving supporter of me, Mother to our children, and Grandmother to our grand-kids the likes of which any man would thank God for.

Two other men have been instrumental in completing this project. My son-in-law, Dr. Thomas H. Noyes, along with his moral support and encouragement spent hours helping to proofread the text and give suggestions to help improve its quality. Dr. William C. Class, my former Pastor, provided help with research, gave me encouragement, and most importantly helped me move my ideas from a manuscript to a finished book. To both these men, I am most grateful.

Finally, to you the reader, I also extend my thanks. Thank you for having the desire to have a greater understanding of God's enduring promises to his children. Please approach this work with an open mind and a humble spirit, which is the same characteristic with which it was written. Whether you agree or disagree with everything in this book, I pray that it may serve as an instrument to challenge you toward a greater understanding of God's Word.

Jesus Christ the same yesterday, and to day, and for ever.
Heb 13:8

INTRODUCTION

GOD is Speaking to America

> [12] Blessed is the nation whose God is the LORD; and the people whom he hath chosen for his own inheritance. Psalms 33:12

Surely, God has blessed this nation as no other. These blessings come through an unconditional promise made to Abraham, Isaac, Jacob and through Joseph and his two sons Ephraim and Manasseh. These blessings of wealth, prosperity and power has been poured out on our great nation more than any other nation on earth.

Great men, on their knees, sought the wisdom of God. He responded and said, "Blessed". These great men and their trust in God have faded from the tapestry of the landscape of the riches, prosperity and power that we received from his generous hand.

God also speaks to us in another place and it is a dire warning we face today, because we have turned from his guidance. "I will break the pride of your power" Lev. 26:19. Does this sound like the situation we are in today? With the greatest military power in the world, we cannot stop a single crazy terrorist from killing hundreds, even thousands of our own innocent citizens. Millions live in fear of the next diabolical attack. Our elected officials in Washington, and every seat of authority, fight each other for individual power and position and are incapable of any form of leadership for the common good. Blood flows from our streets and the abortion clinics. Filth pours from our television screens and the mouths of our children. Anger and violence spreads across our land in the name of free speech. God is angry and if there were tears in Heaven Christ would be weeping.

If God's promises to bless came true, his promises to destroy will also come to pass. There is one more promise that we might still have time to claim.

If my people, which are called by my name, shall humble themselves, and pray, and seek my face, and turn from their wicked ways; then will I hear from heaven, and will forgive their sin, and will heal their land 2 Chron 7:14 (KJV).

THE BIRTHRIGHT AND THE BLESSING: DESTINED FOR GREATNESS

> ⁸ And I heard, but I understood not: then said I, O my Lord, what *shall be* the end of these *things?* ⁹ And he said, Go thy way, Daniel: for the words *are* closed up and sealed till the time of the end. ¹⁰ Many shall be purified, and made white, and tried; but the wicked shall do wickedly: and none of the wicked shall understand; but the wise shall understand.
> Dan 12:8-10

What a great place to start searching the scriptures to understand God's Word. We begin by looking at Daniel's prophecy where God reveals that complete understanding remains closed (kept secret) until the time when the end (Last Days) nears. If we are indeed in the Last Days, as many contend and scripture points to, then God expects the wise to understand secrets that until now have remained a mystery.

This passage clearly teaches that one of the most pivotal books of prophecy (Daniel) was not written to the Ancient Kingdoms of Israel or Judah. In fact, Israel had already ceased to be a nation approximately 300 years before Daniel's writing (721 – 718 BC) and Judah was in Babylonian captivity as Daniel is writing. It was imposed on Judah when Nebuchadnezzar's Army conquered it over a period of 19 years (604-585 BC). The principles and precepts taught in the book are true for all people in all times, however the full prophetic message of Daniel is not written to the past, but to the future. The passing of each day brings the future closer to becoming the present, and our understanding of scripture mandates that we view many prophecies as pointing to our own time. So let us begin with the point of view that we are living in the Last Days and therefore we are expected to gain a more complete understanding of prophecy.

So Where Did the Promise of Spiritual Blessings and National Greatness Begin?

We start by tracing the beginning of the promises of Spiritual Blessings and National Greatness made to the people of Hebrew ancestry.[1] Even more important than tracing the roots of the promise, is to consider whether or not these promises achieved fulfillment? If they are already completed, then where and to whom do we find the reality of that fulfillment manifested today? When prophecy finds fulfillment in events of the past, we must place it into the category of history, not prophecy.

To discover the history of these promises, we begin at Genesis 12:1 and find an amazing encounter between God and Man.

> [1] Now the LORD had said unto Abram, Get thee out of thy country, and from thy kindred, and from thy father's house, unto a land that I will shew thee: [2] And I will make of thee a great nation, and I will bless thee, and make thy name great; and thou shalt be a blessing: [3] And I will bless them that bless thee, and curse him that curseth thee: and in thee shall all families of the earth be blessed. Gen 12:1-3

Verse 4 shows the simple response of faith by Abram, "So Abram departed." There was an immediate response

---

[1] Material Blessings – those blessings typified by the promise to make Abraham's heirs a great nation.

Spiritual Blessings – blessings typified by the promise to bless all nations through the heirs of Abraham and become a blessing to all nations through Christ.

in complete obedience by Abram. God saw a man whom he could use as a channel for his blessings to all mankind for the next 4000 years. This in spite of the fact that a pagan family who worshipped other gods had raised him. (See Joshua 24:2-3) We find two thousand years of human history recorded in the first eleven chapters of Genesis. However, here in the first three verses of chapter 12, the Almighty God lays the foundation for over four thousand years of his mercy and blessings to all mankind.

The Lord gave Abram a mandate that was conditional at the time. He embarks on a trip of faith, leaving the land of his birth and journeying into a strange land of God's own choosing. In five short statements God's promises covered His unimaginable blessing, foreknowledge and plan for all the people of God. He said:

- I will bless thee
- I will make thy name great
- You will be a blessing
- I will bless them that bless you
- All of the families of the earth will be blessed thru you

Nothing else in the entire Bible compares to the historical scope and magnitude of these verses. Our minds cannot begin to comprehend the far-reaching implications of this condensed form of God's Blessings. However, God has provided expanded clarity and insight throughout His Word and "the wise shall understand," as he promised to Daniel.

Later, by investigating the details of His word completely, these promises unfold before our eyes. The extent to which God uses Abram to bless the entire human race is clear and concise. As the picture unfolds, it becomes quite evident that God's ways are not our ways. Furthermore, from a human perspective, it seems as if God displays a sense of humor in choosing a man most unqualified for the task before him. Consider this: in Abram, he had just chosen a man who was:

- Of a pagan background
- At the time of his calling was already seventy-five years old
- Had a wife known to be barren
- Both were well beyond normal child-bearing ages

However, remember that he declares to us "His ways are not our ways."

> ⁹ Remember the former things of old: for I am God, and there is none else; I am God, and there is none like me,
>
> ¹⁰ Declaring the end from the beginning, and from ancient times the things that are not yet done, saying, My counsel shall stand, and I will do all my pleasure   Isaiah 46:9-10

Abraham's Obedience

Continuing now in Genesis chapter 12, verse 4.

> ⁴ So Abram departed, as the LORD had spoken unto him; and Lot went with him: and Abram *was* seventy and five years old when he departed out of Haran. ⁵ And Abram took Sarai his wife, and Lot his brother's son, and all their substance that they had gathered, and the souls that they had gotten in Haran; and they went forth to go into the land of Canaan; and into the land of Canaan they came.   Gen 12:4-5

Abram would later demonstrate fairness and generosity to Lot in Genesis 13 and honor to the king of Salem. Character traits God desired when he first called him. However, Abram was yet to demonstrate his most admirable characteristic, faith! Abram's first act of faith was not on that hilltop with Isaac, his first step of faith was to leave from where he was to where God wanted him to be. When he departed Haran, he was acting in faith.

Promises Expanded : Protector - Provider

> ¹ After these things the word of the LORD came unto Abram in a vision, saying, Fear not, Abram: I *am* thy shield, *and* thy exceeding great reward. ² And Abram said, Lord GOD, what wilt thou give me, seeing I go childless, and the steward of my house *is* this Eliezer of Damascus? Gen 15:1-2

To paraphrase, Abram asked God, "Just how are you going to do all of this? I have no heirs, I am old, my wife is old and barren, and the only trusted person I have is a pagan Syrian who works for me." As always, God has an answer to our questions, doubts, and fears.

> ⁴ And, behold, the word of the LORD *came* unto him, saying, This shall not be thine heir; but he that shall come forth out of thine own bowels shall be thine heir.
>
> ⁵ And he brought him forth abroad, and said, Look now toward heaven, and tell the stars, if thou be able to number them: and he said unto him, So shall thy seed be. ⁶ And he believed in the LORD; and he counted it to him for righteousness. Gen 15:4-6
>
> ¹⁸ In the same day the LORD made a covenant with Abram, saying, Unto thy seed have I given this land, from the river of Egypt unto the great river, the river Euphrates: Gen 15:18

In these passages, God sets the boundaries in an everlasting Covenant to all of God's people. Because it lasts forever, it becomes the place of eternal rule of Christ in the millennium. Read in Ezekiel chapters 40 through 48 to find a good example of this truth.

Moving forward to chapter seventeen in Genesis:

> ¹ And when Abram was ninety years old and nine, the LORD appeared to Abram, and said unto him, I *am* the Almighty God; walk before me, and be thou perfect. ² And I will make my covenant between me and thee, and will multiply thee exceedingly. ³ And Abram fell on his face: and God talked with him, saying,
>
> ⁴ As for me, behold, my covenant *is* with thee, and thou shalt be a father of many nations. ⁵ Neither shall thy name any more be called Abram, but thy name shall be Abraham; for a father of many nations have I made thee.
>
> ⁶ And I will make thee exceeding fruitful, and I will make nations of thee, and kings shall come out of thee. ⁷ And I will establish my covenant between me and thee and thy seed after thee in their generations for an everlasting covenant, to be a God unto thee, and to thy seed after thee. ⁸ And I will give unto thee, and to thy seed after thee, the land wherein thou art a stranger, all the land of Canaan, for an everlasting possession; and I will be their God. ⁹ And God said unto Abraham, Thou shalt keep my covenant therefore, thou, and thy seed after thee in their generations. ¹⁰ This *is* my covenant, which ye shall keep, between me and you and thy seed after thee; Every man child among you shall be circumcised   Gen 17:1-10

Here the Lord appears to Abram, further expanding and clarifying his promise.

- I will multiply thee exceedingly – v.2
- You shall be a father of many nations - v.4
- Thy name shall be Abraham – v.5
- I will make thee exceedingly fruitful – v.6
- Kings shall come out of thee – v.6
- I will establish my covenant for an everlasting covenant with thee and thy seed after thee – v.7

- The land of Canaan shall be an everlasting possession – v.8

We must understand that the action in these verses takes place some sixteen years after Abram's call in chapter 12. By this time, Ishmael had already been born to Hagar the Egyptian in Abram's haste to run ahead of God. Now God confirms his blessings would come thru his wife, Sarah. This intervention by God shows Isaac to be the true heir. God makes his will known by identifying Sara as the channel of his blessings.

- He changed her name to Sarah – v.15
- She (not Hagar) would be a mother of nations – v.16
- Kings and people shall be of him – v.16
- Provisions are made for Ishmael to receive a blessing also (including having twelve princes as heirs – v.20

Genesis, chapter 21, becomes a highlight of God's working in Abraham and Sarah through the birth of Isaac, the true heir. Chapter 22 brings the reader to the pivotal event in the entire plan for the promises God made to Abraham. Again, God expands and clarifies His promises not just in word, but also in action. Most importantly, the promises become <u>unconditional</u>. A most beautiful picture emerges as we watch the faith of Abraham become a foundation of blessings for all people and a vision of God's own sacrifice in Jesus. It will take centuries for God's plans to unfold. The unconditional nature of the promised blessings, carried out in spite of Abraham's seed falling away from God, proves to be true. Despite sin and disobedience, the fulfillment of the eternal plan of God remains with the heirs of Abraham.

Several scriptural truths require examination if we are to understand the fulfillment of God's promise and blessings. Truths made clear through prophets, who later confirm God's hand at work in the completion of His plan. Here we introduce two key terms, the "material blessings," and the "spiritual blessings." Terms used to describe the nature of God's blessings and promises made to Abraham and his seed.

The initial promises made to Abram in Chapter 12 were conditional on Abram's obedience to get out of the Ur of the Chaldeans, away from the pagan gods and follow the true God. In 17:1&2, God places another condition on Abraham, along with a reaffirmation of the promise.

> [1] And when Abram was ninety years old and nine, the LORD appeared to Abram, and said unto him, I *am* the Almighty God; walk before me, and be thou perfect. [2] And I will make my covenant between me and thee, and will multiply thee exceedingly.   Gen 17:1-2

However, in chapter 22, when Abraham is about to offer Isaac as a sacrifice according to God's instructions, suddenly God stayed his hand. It is as if God is saying, "you have done enough to prove yourself." Now Abraham has shown himself to be trustworthy, he has earned the blessings God promised as a part of the Covenant. Now God will keep his promise and pour out the material and spiritual blessings to Abraham and his heirs. Until the end of the ages, each generation will benefit from Abraham's faithful response to God.

> [15] And the angel of the LORD called unto Abraham out of heaven the second time, [16] And said, By myself have I sworn, saith the LORD, for because thou hast done this thing, and hast not withheld thy son, thine only *son*:

¹⁷ That in blessing I will bless thee, and in multiplying I will multiply thy seed as the stars of the heaven, and as the sand which *is* upon the sea shore; and thy seed shall possess the gate of his enemies; **¹⁸** And in thy seed shall all the nations of the earth be blessed; because thou hast obeyed my voice. Gen 22:15-18

"Because thou hast done this thing," what a tremendous, all encompassing and unconditional promise God made to Abraham. We begin to see the scope of what God was to perform through the life of one obedient man. The promises to include the tremendous spiritual and material blessings, *"I will multiply they seed as the stars of the heaven"*, would seem in light of future scriptures, this promise acts as a reference to the worldwide spiritual blessings in store for all future generations from Abraham through Christ to all people through Judah. *"And as the sands which is upon the sea shore,"* seems to refer to the worldwide material blessings promised through Joseph. *"Thy seed shall possess the gates of his enemies."* In the Fraternal Blessings of Genesis 25, Abraham passes these blessings to his son Isaac. *"And Abraham gave all that he had unto Isaac"* Gen 25:4-5.

Ishmael, the son of Hagar, had been expelled from the household of Abraham along with his mother. With the expulsion however came a promise that he also would become a nation. The promise based upon the fact that Ishmael was also Abraham's seed (Gen. 21:12-13) Interestingly, only Ishmael was given this extra promise, all the rest of the children of Abraham by his concubines were simply given a one-time gift and dismissed from the camp.

⁶ But unto the sons of the concubines, which Abraham had, Abraham gave gifts, and sent them away from Isaac his son, while he yet lived, eastward, unto the east country. Gen 25:6

While Isaac is given all as a birthright, Ishmael is to become a nation. What kind of a nation does God have in store for Ishmael to become the father of? Before his birth, his mother Hagar has an encounter with God in which we find a character sketch of Ishmael and his descendants. The angel of the Lord appears to Hagar in the desert. He gives her guidance and reveals to her the plan God has for her yet to be born son.

> [10] And the angel of the LORD said unto her, I will multiply thy seed exceedingly, that it shall not be numbered for multitude. [11] And the angel of the LORD said unto her, Behold, thou *art* with child, and shalt bear a son, and shalt call his name Ishmael; because the LORD hath heard thy affliction. [12] And he will be a wild man; his hand *will be* against every man, and every man's hand against him; and he shall dwell in the presence of all his brethren.   Gen 16:10-12

It is well to take note what God said about the future generations of Ishmael.

- Become a Nation of people
- Be a wild man
- Hand would be against every man
- Every man's hand would be against him
- Would dwell in the presence of his brethren

Remember that Ishmael was of Egyptian blood through his mother Hagar. With these prophecies along with other scriptural references and historical events, we can see a nation with these characteristics emerge.

1. A Nation of Egyptian ancestry (through Hagar)
2. Dwelling first in the middle east
3. Later dwelling among the house of Israel (the

birthright nation)
4. Acting out their wild nature through such characteristics as murder and destruction

This is the nation that Ishmael was to father. Not a dead nation found only on an old map, rather a nation that continues to this day with these characteristics, as its general national identity. When we apply these national characteristics, one people stand out. The Nation of Islam, with its false religion fits this prophecy. (Interesting that only the Islamic people are referred to as the "Nation of Islam" without regard to any geographical location) They are a nation with no boundaries, a wild people bent on death and destruction. They are carrying out their ancestral heritage. Their hand is against every man, and every man's hand moves against them. They dwell among their brethren, those who have the blessing of being the true birthright. Current events serve only to testify to the truth of God's Words to Hagar. Ishmael has become a nation that grew up alongside, yet removed from the blessings of God's people. Even as the believers of Islam contend they are the rightful recipients of the birthright of Abraham, history reveals a different reality. Historically, a warring people who seek to live among others (their brethren), yet death and destruction seem to be their calling card.

THE NEXT GENERATION - ISAAC TAKES A WIFE

Abraham was now ready to die and called his eldest servant for a special task. Abraham charged his servant requiring him to take an oath of dedication to complete the will of Abraham. Within the oath, Abraham outlines his instructions. Isaac's wife will not come from the daughters of the Canaanites but rather from among the daughters of his kinsmen. This means a journey back to the land we know as Mesopotamia, the ancient land of Ur. Also within the oath, Abraham assured his servant that God would send his Angel before him, directing him to the wife God had chosen for Isaac. (Gen. 24:1-5) As a result of honoring his commitment, the servant discovers Rebekah by following God's direction. A choice ultimately confirmed by her brother, Laban, as he pronounces his blessing on Rebekah and the pending marriage.

> They blessed Rebekah, saying to her: Our sister, may you become upon ten thousands. May your offspring possess gates of their enemies. Gen 24:60 (HCSB)

Furthermore, God gives Rebekah an assurance and confirmation of his will by proclaiming to her the blessings of her future offspring.

> And the LORD said to her: Two nations are in your womb; two people will [come] from you and be separated. One people will be stronger than the other, and the older will serve the younger. Gen 25:23 (HCSB)

The events of chapter 26 & 27 detail the early life of Esau the oldest and Jacob the youngest. Jacob stole the birthright, which had to do with earthly blessings. He then received the blessings that had to do with spiritual things from his father, Isaac². This encompassed the material blessings already detailed, and as we shall see, is expanded and clarified in many other scriptures.

> Esau now returns with his offering to his father, Isaac, and asks for his blessing. This is recorded in Gen. 27:30-40. Paraphrasing, Isaac tells him, "too late, I have given all the blessings (including the birthright that was rightly Esau's) to your brother." In response to Esau's pleading for one remaining blessing, Isaac proclaims a blessing less than overwhelming.
>
> ³⁹ And Isaac his father answered and said unto him, Behold, thy dwelling shall be the fatness of the earth, and of the dew of heaven from above; ⁴⁰ And by thy sword shalt thou live, and shalt serve thy brother; and it shall come to pass when thou shalt have the dominion, that thou shalt break his yoke from off thy neck.   Gen 27:39-40
>
> ³⁹ Then his father Isaac answered him: Look, your dwelling place will be from the richness of the land, from the dew of the sky above.   ⁴⁰ You will live by your sword,   you will serve your brother. But when you rebel, will break his yoke from your neck. Gen 27:39-40 (HCSB)

Here, the Holman translation, as well as other translations, gives a better translation of the Hebrew text. Isaac is not blessing Esau with the fatness of the earth; rather he is going to live by the sword in service to his brother. He will live away from the fatness of the earth and the dew of the sky. Esau, later removing himself from Jacob, moving himself, his family, and his household to the hill country proves this translation. (Gen. 36:6,7) The

---

² Therefore God give thee of the dew of heaven, and the fatness of the earth, and plenty of corn and wine: Let people serve thee, and nations bow down to thee: be Lord over thy brethren, and let thy mother's sons bow down to thee: cursed be every one that curseth thee, and blessed be he that blesseth thee.   Gen 27:28-29

result of the selling of the birthright by Esau to Jacob, and the tricking of Isaac to give his blessing to Jacob, is that both the spiritual and material blessings passed on to Jacob alone. The possession of both these blessing by only one man lasts only one generation. The next generation experiences a change where both blessings are not in the possession of just one man.

JACOB'S TWELVE SONS

¹ And Isaac called Jacob, and blessed him, and charged him, and said unto him, Thou shalt not take a wife of the daughters of Canaan. ² Arise, go to Padanaram, to the house of Bethuel thy mother's father; and take thee a wife from thence of the daughters of Laban thy mother's brother. ³ And God Almighty bless thee, and make thee fruitful, and multiply thee, that thou mayest be a multitude of people; ⁴ And give thee the blessing of Abraham, to thee, and to thy seed with thee; that thou mayest inherit the land wherein thou art a stranger, which God gave unto Abraham.   Gen 28:1-4

¹⁴ And thy seed shall be as the dust of the earth, and thou shalt spread abroad to the west, and to the east, and to the north, and to the south: and in thee and in thy seed shall all the families of the earth be blessed.   Gen 28:14

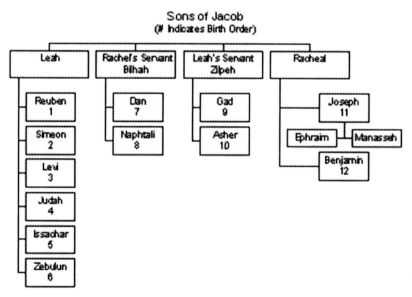

Jacob followed his father's instructions and journeyed to the east where he found Laban's family. The first person he saw was Rachel, and he knew she was the one he was to marry. This marriage in the future would enable him to fulfill God's promise to Abraham to make him the father of many people.

> [11] And Jacob kissed Rachel, and lifted up his voice, and wept. [12] And Jacob told Rachel that he *was* her father's brother, and that he *was* Rebekah's son: and she ran and told her father. [13] And it came to pass, when Laban heard the tidings of Jacob his sister's son, that he ran to meet him, and embraced him, and kissed him, and brought him to his house. Gen 29:10-13

Jacob promised to serve Laban seven years for the hand of Rachel, the wife to whom God had led him. However, Laban had other plans for the price of Rachel's hand. After seven years of servitude for Rachel, Laban substituted his oldest daughter Leah. The price for Rachel's hand would now be taking Leah as a wife and then serving another seven years. While serving those seven years to obtain the wife God desired for Jacob, Leah bore him six sons. (In order of birth - Reuben, Simeon, Levi, Judah, Issachar and Zebulum) It is noteworthy to pause here and emphasis how the sons fit into God's plan. We find this information in Genesis 49, prophetic scriptures that point to the future of their lineage.

> [1] And Jacob called unto his sons, and said, Gather yourselves together, that I may tell you *that* which shall befall you in the Last Days. Gen 49:1

The follow is a commentary on Jacob's words to each of his sons.

Reuben: The first born, and was by custom the recipient of the inherited birthright. The birthright encompassed most the material blessings (owned material property) by the father. However, Jacob disqualifies Ruben from being the recipient for two reasons. One is obvious in nature, the other not so obvious until later in history. First, Ruben was not Rachel's son. Jacob understood that Rachel was the woman God had chosen for him to bear the heir of the blessings. As a result, Jacob relegated the sons of Leah to a secondary position. Secondly, Ruben further disqualified himself by committing incest with his father's (concubine) wife. (Genesis 35:22) This disqualification is outlined in 1 Chronicles 5:1, dispelling any doubt about Jacobs decision. " *Now the sons of Reuben the firstborn of Israel, (for he was the firstborn; but, forasmuch as he defiled his father's bed, his birthright was given unto the sons of Joseph the son of Israel: and the genealogy is not to be reckoned after the birthright. 1 Chron 5:1*"

Simeon: One of the lesser characters in God's plan, Jacob deals harshly with him. Jacob calls him an instrument of cruelty (Gen. 49:5) and curses his fierce anger (vs. 7). The plight of Simeon's lineage is that that of being divided and scattered.

Levi: In Genesis 49, Levi shared a heritage with Simeon because they shared in the sin of incest. Their punishment is recorded also in Deuteronomy 27:20. However, in later generations the lineage of Levi finds redemption. Moses, under the guidance of God, recognized in the Levitical line a divine responsibility. Through the appointment of Aaron of the Tribe of Levi, all future generation receive a blessing in being elevated to the priestly line. (Exodus 4:14)

Judah: Later scriptures identify Judah as the tribe from which Christ would be born. The line of Judah, through Christ, serves as the ultimate fulfillment of God's promises to Abraham, Isaac, and Jacob. This blessing brings about the greatest promise for which the world and humanity could ever hope. This blessing is the embodiment of the spiritual blessing, apart from the material blessing. Note that the words spoken to Judah are those of praise and promise. His name means, "praise Yahweh." The "scepter," also mentioned in Genesis 49 as a part of

Judah's blessing, is a sign of the spiritual blessing. The scepter is completely separate from the material blessings and symbolizes the spiritual blessing.

Zebulun: This fifth son of Jacob receives a blessing of a portion of the Promised Land, however, Jacob says little else regarding him. His dwelling place near the sea indicates a lifestyle consistent with seaman. This tribe, referenced in several Old Testament passages, none of which deals specifically with the tribe being a part of either the Birthright or the Scepter blessings. However he as all other tribes participate indirectly.

Issachar: Apparently he was a rebellious son of which little is said. In his last will and testament, Jacob describes him as "strong ass" destined to be a servant unto tribute. Not much of a legacy, a tribe of hard workers, slaves to money. However, the heirs are recognized in Judges as one of the tribes who supported Deborah (Judges 5:16).

Sons of Haste: Rebekah, Jacob's true love, was for a while barren. A condition she shared with her mother-in-law, Rachel and her grandmother-in-law, Elizabeth. Rebekah became angry and jealous of Leah, desiring to give her husband a son. Like Sarah, her initial solution was to give her handmaiden, Bilhah, to Jacob to mother a son in her place. Out of that union came two sons, Dan and Naphtali.

Dan: When Jacob spoke to Dan on his deathbed, he prophesied that Dan would be one of the Judges in the tribes of Israel. (Gen. 49:16) He followed that prophecy with a strange statement. "Dan shall be a serpent by the way." These are not idle words. As all of God's Words, including those spoken by his messengers, as Jacob is here, they do have meaning and purpose. This description of Dan later reveals the prophetic nature of this phrase.

<u>Naphtali:</u> Meaning, "Wresting with God," lives as a constant reminder of Rebekah's conflict with her sister. The second of Jacob and Bilhah's sons, he too gives the appearance of being passive in God's plan for his people. Like Dan, however, his linage shows up more prominently in later scripture. The importance of Dan and Naphtali to God's overall later plans plays into the discussion of following chapters.

<u>Asher:</u> see below

RACHEL

<u>Zillah:</u> Not allowing ~~Rebekah~~ to outdo her, Leah provides her handmaiden to Jacob to bear two more sons. These two sons represent a renewed hope that Jacob will favor her and her sons upon his death. Note that she claims a promise that is not hers to make. *" 13 And Leah said, Happy am I, for the daughters will call me blessed: and she called his name Asher."* Gen 30:13. God had previously confirmed that blessing in Sarah[3], Rebecca[4], and Rachel[5].

<u>Sons of Promise:</u> Sons given to Rachel by God when he remembers her plight and opens her womb.

<u>Joseph:</u> See following pages.

<u>Benjamin:</u> These two "Sons of Promise" are the primary subjects of the next chapter. A complete description of their blessings from Jacob and their place in God's plan is discussed there.

---

[3] Genesis 17:16
[4] Genesis 24:6
[5] Through her first born son – Joseph – Genesis 49:22=28

> ²² And God remembered Rachel, and God hearkened to her, and opened her womb. ²³ And she conceived, and bare a son; and said, God hath taken away my reproach: ²⁴ And she called his name Joseph; and said, The LORD shall add to me another son. Gen 30:22-24

Later, Rachel gave birth to Jacob's twelfth son Benjamin, only to die in childbirth.

> ¹⁷ And it came to pass, when she was in hard labour, that the midwife said unto her, Fear not; thou shalt have this son also. ¹⁸ And it came to pass, as her soul was in departing, (for she died) that she called his name Benoni: but his father called him Benjamin. ¹⁹ And Rachel died, and was buried in the way to Ephrath, which *is* Bethlehem. ²⁰ And Jacob set a pillar upon her grave: that *is* the pillar of Rachel's grave unto this day. Gen 35:17-20

Walking With a Limp

After Jocob grew into manhood, God needed to get his attention. Similar to how God needed to get the attention of his father Isaac and his grandfather Abraham before him. Jacob was on his way to an encounter with Esau, his estranged brother, when God stepped in. He found himself wrestling with an angel who blessed him, crippled him, and changed his name, all as a way of preparing him for a real encounter with God.

> ²⁴ And Jacob was left alone; and there wrestled a man with him until the breaking of the day. ²⁵ And when he saw that he prevailed not against him, he touched the hollow of his thigh; and the hollow of Jacob's thigh was out of joint, as he wrestled with him. ²⁶ And he said, Let me go, for the day breaketh. And he said, I will not let thee go, except thou bless me. ²⁷ And he said unto him, What *is* thy name? And

he said, Jacob. ²⁸ And he said, Thy name shall be called no more Jacob, but Israel: for as a prince hast thou power with God and with men, and hast prevailed.

²⁹ And Jacob asked *him*, and said, Tell *me*, I pray thee, thy name. And he said, Wherefore *is* it *that* thou dost ask after my name? And he blessed him there. ³⁰ And Jacob called the name of the place Peniel: for I have seen God face to face, and my life is preserved. ³¹ And as he passed over Penuel the sun rose upon him, and he halted upon his thigh. Gen 32:24-31

The encounter reminds us that, like Jacob, after we wrestle with God, we always walk with a limp and not in our own strength. His purpose is to draw us back to himself. In Genesis 35:1, God calls Jacob to go to Bethel, dwell there, and make an altar to God. Further details of this encounter with God are detailed in "The Throne of David" and "The History of the Rock: Jacob's Pillow," later chapters of this book.

⁹ And God appeared unto Jacob again, when he came out of Padanaram, and blessed him. ¹⁰ And God said unto him, Thy name *is* Jacob: thy name shall not be called any more Jacob, but Israel shall be thy name: and he called his name Israel. ¹¹ And God said unto him, I *am* God Almighty: be fruitful and multiply; a nation and a company of nations shall be of thee, and kings shall come out of thy loins; ¹² And the land which I gave Abraham and Isaac, to thee I will give it, and to thy seed after thee will I give the land Gen 35:9-12

It is in this situation that God confirms the promises he had made to Abraham and Isaac now extend to Jacob. To Jacob, God expanded the original promises by revealing that not only shall he be the father of nations, but a company of nations. These are material blessings in addition to those promised to Abraham and Isaac, amazingly prophesied by God Almighty. These promises come without any conditions placed upon Jacob by God.

Fast forward to the time when Israel (Jacob) is an old man. Many events have highlighted his life since the time of receiving God's Blessing at Bethel. Consider this very brief/simplified outline of events, which occur during the life of Jacob.

- Joseph, his favorite son, first born of the promise (as later confirmed in scripture) has been hated by all his half-brother's, sold into slavery, and assumed dead
- Joseph, through the protection of God, found favor in the eyes of Pharaoh, is elevated to the position of second in command in Egypt
- A major drought in the Mediterranean region leads to an area-wide famine, yet under the guidance of Joseph, Egypt avoids disaster and has enough food storage to supply surrounding peoples
- Following two excursions into Egypt by Jacob's sons (Benjamin on the second only) to purchase food, Joseph made himself known to his half-brothers and sent for his father, Jacob
- Jacob moved his family and possessions to Goshen,· near Egypt

---

* Go´shen. - The name of a part of Egypt where the Israelites dwelt during the whole period of their sojourn in that country. It was probably situated on the eastern border of the Nile, extending from the Mediterranean to the Red Sea. It contained the treasure-cities of Rameses and Pittim. It was a pasture land, especially suited to a shepherd people, and sufficient for the Israelites, who there prospered, and were separate from the main body of the Egyptians.

- Jacob's reunion with his son Joseph was a time of Joy and great thanksgiving
- Jacob prospered in the land of Egypt to the extent that only the Divine Hand of God can account for
- It is here in Egypt that the covenant promise of God is handed down from Jacob to the sons of Joseph

The Line Continues

> [20] And unto Joseph in the land of Egypt were born Manasseh and Ephraim, which Asenath the daughter of Potipherah priest of On bare unto him. Gen 46:20

Note these sons were born into the promised birthright line, however they were half Egyptian and something had to be done to make them true Israelites. An amazing event took place before Jacob died which would bring Manasseh and Ephraim into the fold.

> [1] And it came to pass after these things, that *one* told Joseph, Behold, thy father *is* sick: and he took with him his two sons, Manasseh and Ephraim. [2] And *one* told Jacob, and said, Behold, thy son Joseph cometh unto thee: and Israel strengthened himself, and sat upon the bed. Gen 48:1-2

We discover the use of interesting phrasing in this sequence of passages. A messenger is introduced identified simply as "one". The distinction used twice, once to inform Joseph of Jacob's condition, and once to inform Jacob of Joseph's arrival. Are we being introduced to one person, two people, or simply to insignificant messenger(s)? It can be very tempting to try to find a parallel between these two individuals and the angels who had visited Abraham. However, the reference in this passage is simply too vague to make any such claim. Then in 2b, the designation of

Jacob changes to Israel, the name that God had bestowed upon him at the time of covenant confirmation.

This is not a vague or random change; rather it emphasizes the accuracy of God's Word. Israel was preparing himself to pass on the blessing to Joseph and his sons. As a man, Jacob had wrestled with God so long ago; he was not qualified to pass on the heritage of God's blessings. Israel, the man changed by his all night wrestling encounter with God, possesses a unique qualification. In the presence of God, Jacob ceases to exist. Instead, God changes this man so completely that a new name is required. God makes Jacob a new man by changing his name. Jacob means "the one who follows on the heals of another," or, "the one who supplants." So complete did the encounter with God change him that God renamed him "Israel"; which means, "Wrestles with God" or "Prevailed against God". The importance of passing along the blessings of God to the rightful heirs requires the proclamation comes from Israel, not Jacob. The blessings come not from a person who supplants another (Jacob), but from a man who has been in the very presence of God and received the blessing first hand from Him (Israel).

The Line is Strengthened

> ³ And Jacob said unto Joseph, God Almighty appeared unto me at Luz in the land of Canaan, and blessed me, ⁴ And said unto me, Behold, I will make thee fruitful, and multiply thee, and I will make of thee a multitude of people; and will give this land to thy seed after thee *for* an everlasting possession. ⁵ And now thy two sons, Ephraim and Manasseh, which were born unto thee in the land of Egypt before I came unto thee into Egypt, *are* mine; as Reuben and Simeon, they shall be mine. Gen 48:3-5

Israel adopted Joseph's two sons and placed his name Israel upon them. Furthermore, he placed them at the head of the inheritance line as his first and second born. In doing so, he supplants his first two sons, who were born to Leah. These two grandsons are substitutes for the men who would normally be in line to receive the blessings of Israel. The actions and event that take place at the side of Israel as he lies on his deathbed are much more than propagating family traditions. They take on the stature of prophecy, perhaps as important as any other prophecy found in scripture. They become a prophetic picture of God's adoption of those who join themselves to him by the faithful actions of His own son. Much like Joseph, Jesus presents Himself to God. They receive the blessings of the Father based purely on the introduction of them by the Son. The heritage blessings of the Father are passed along to those who are undeserving, those who are adopted into the Family and placed in a position of honor because of the redemptive work of the son.

> [17] And if children, then heirs; heirs of God, and joint-heirs with Christ; if so be that we suffer with *him*, that we may be also glorified together

> [25] As he saith also in Osee, I will call them my people, which were not my people; and her beloved, which was not beloved. [26] And it shall come to pass, *that* in the place where it was said unto them, Ye *are* not my people; there shall they be called the children of the living God.   Romans 8:17 & Romans 9:25-26

As the writer of Romans points out, this same type of substitution and adoption is at work in God's gift of salvation to a people who are undeserving. The actions of Israel in blessing the sons of Joseph, in essence adopting them and lifting them to a position of supplanting the traditional heirs, is nothing short of a prophetic picture of salvation through faith in Jesus.

> ⁶ And thy issue, which thou begettest after them, shall be thine, *and* shall be called after the name of their brethren in their inheritance. Gen 48:6

Israel clarifies the fact that Ephraim and Manasseh are indeed set apart from the rest of Joseph's children. They will receive the blessings of the first born as if they were Jacob's very own children, allotting their brothers an inheritance in keeping with the other brothers. The birthright, and all it represents, is the possession of these two alone and the tribes they represent. Chapter 48 of Genesis further clarifies and confirms this birthright line.

> ⁸ And Israel beheld Joseph's sons, and said, Who are these? ⁹ And Joseph said unto his father, They are my sons, whom God hath given me in this place. And he said, Bring them, I pray thee, unto me, and I will bless them. ¹⁰ Now the eyes of Israel were dim for age, so that he could not see. And he brought them near unto him; and he kissed them, and embraced them.
>
> ¹¹ And Israel said unto Joseph, I had not thought to see thy face: and, lo, God hath shewed me also thy seed. ¹² And Joseph brought them out from between his knees, and he bowed himself with his face to the earth. ¹³ And Joseph took them both, Ephraim in his right hand toward Israel's left hand, and Manasseh in his left hand toward Israel's right hand, and brought them near unto him. ¹⁴ And Israel stretched out his right hand, and laid it upon Ephraim's head, who was the younger, and his left hand upon Manasseh's head, guiding his hands wittingly; for Manasseh was the firstborn. ¹⁵ And he blessed Joseph, and said, God, before whom my fathers Abraham and Isaac did walk, the God which fed me all my life long unto this day, ¹⁶ The Angel which redeemed me from all evil, bless the lads; and let my name be named on them, and the name of my fathers Abraham and Isaac; and let them grow into a multitude in the midst of the earth. ¹⁷ And when Joseph

saw that his father laid his right hand upon the head of Ephraim, it displeased him: and he held up his father's hand, to remove it from Ephraim's head unto Manasseh's head. ¹⁸ And Joseph said unto his father, Not so, my father: for this is the firstborn; put thy right hand upon his head. ¹⁹ And his father refused, and said, I know it, my son, I know it: he also shall become a people, and he also shall be great: but truly his younger brother shall be greater than he, and his seed shall become a multitude of nations. ²⁰ And he blessed them that day, saying, In thee shall Israel bless, saying, God make thee as Ephraim and as Manasseh: and he set Ephraim before Manasseh. ²¹ And Israel said unto Joseph, Behold, I die: but God shall be with you, and bring you again unto the land of your fathers. ²² Moreover I have given to thee one portion above thy brethren, which I took out of the hand of the Amorite with my sword and with my bow. Gen 48:8-22

Chapter 48 introduces another change in the inheritance traditions. For the second time in three generations, the inheritance of the birthright bypasses the first-born. The same inheritance irregularity occurred when Jacob, the younger son, received the blessing of his father Isaac over Esau, the older son. In this situation, however, the scope of the inheritance traditions stretches even further because Jacob is not only bypassing the oldest son; he is bypassing the entire generation of his sons and bestows his blessing on his grandson.

As Joseph presented his two sons to Jacob to receive his blessing, Manasseh occupied the position of receiving the blessing from Joseph's right hand and Ephraim on the left. The right hand represented the greatest part of the blessing. What Joseph had supposed to be the proper placement of his sons was not what Israel had in mind. <u>Israel crossed his hands and placed his right hand on Ephraim's head.</u> When Joseph tried to interrupt and question his father's actions, Israel refused Joseph's attempt to have his oldest son receive the blessings of the right hand. Israel, however, knew exactly what he was doing. As Mathew Henry notes, "Jacob acted neither by mistake, nor from a partial affection to one more than the other; but from a spirit of prophecy, and by the Divine counsel."⁶ In verse 19, Israel shares his God given insight by proclaiming both will become great peoples, but the role of the younger is greater than that of the older brother.

Through this action of Israel, the birthright line passes to two sons. Manasseh (the older son) received his blessing and the prophecy that his line becomes a great people (nation). Ephraim, however, as a part of his blessing receives the prophetic vision of Israel that his line becomes not just a people (nation), but "multitude of nations." The preeminence of Ephraim over Manasseh is solidified in verse 20 when Ephraim is set before Manasseh, a symbol of importance and position.

> ¹ And Jacob called unto his sons, and said, Gather yourselves together, that I may tell you *that* which shall befall you in the Last Days. ² Gather yourselves together, and hear, ye sons of Jacob; and hearken unto Israel your father. ³ Reuben, thou *art* my firstborn, my might, and the beginning of my strength, the excellency of dignity, and the excellency of power: ⁴ Unstable as water, thou shalt not excel; because thou wentest up to thy father's bed; then defiledst thou *it*: he went up to my couch.
> ⁵ Simeon and Levi *are* brethren; instruments of cruelty *are in* their habitations. ⁶ O my soul, come not thou into their secret; unto their assembly, mine honour, be not thou united: for in their anger they slew a man, and in their selfwill they digged down a wall. ⁷ Cursed *be* their anger, for *it was* fierce; and their wrath, for it was cruel: I will divide them in Jacob, and scatter them in Israel.

---

⁶ <u>Matthew Henry Concise</u>. Electronic text and markup copyright 1995 by Epiphany Software.

8 Judah, thou *art he* whom thy brethren shall praise: thy hand *shall be* in the neck of thine enemies; thy father's children shall bow down before thee. **9** Judah *is* a lion's whelp: from the prey, my son, thou art gone up: he stooped down, he couched as a lion, and as an old lion; who shall rouse him up? **10** <u>The sceptre shall not depart from Judah, nor a lawgiver from between his feet, until Shiloh come; and unto him *shall* the gathering of the people *be.*</u> **11** Binding his foal unto the vine, and his ass's colt unto the choice vine; he washed his garments in wine, and his clothes in the blood of grapes: **12** His eyes *shall be* red with wine, and his teeth white with milk.

13 Zebulun shall dwell at the haven of the sea; and he *shall be* for an haven of ships; and his border *shall be* unto Zidon. **14** Issachar *is* a strong ass couching down between two burdens: **15** And he saw that rest *was* good, and the land that *it was* pleasant; and bowed his shoulder to bear, and became a servant unto tribute. **16** Dan shall judge his people, as one of the tribes of Israel. **17** Dan shall be a serpent by the way, an adder in the path, that biteth the horse heels, so that his rider shall fall backward. **18** I have waited for thy salvation, O LORD. **19** Gad, a troop shall overcome him: but he shall overcome at the last. **20** Out of Asher his *shall be* fat, and he shall yield royal dainties. **21** Naphtali *is* a hind let loose: he giveth goodly words.

22 <u>Joseph *is* a fruitful bough, *even* a fruitful bough by a well; *whose* branches run over the wall: **23** The archers have sorely grieved him, and shot *at him,* and hated him: **24** But his bow abode in strength, and the arms of his hands were made strong by the hands of the mighty *God* of Jacob; (from thence *is* the shepherd, the stone of Israel:) **25** *Even* by the God of thy father, who shall help thee; and by the Almighty, who shall bless thee with blessings of heaven above, blessings of the deep that lieth under, blessings of the breasts, and of the womb: **26** The blessings of thy father have prevailed above the blessings of my progenitors unto the utmost bound of the everlasting hills: they shall be on the head of Joseph, and on the crown of the head of him that was separate from his brethren.</u> **27**

<u>Benjamin</u> shall ravin *as* a wolf: in the morning he shall devour the prey, and at night he shall divide the spoil.

28 All these *are* the twelve tribes of Israel: and this *is it* that their father spake unto them, and blessed them; every

29

one according to his blessing he blessed them. ²⁹ And he charged them, and said unto them, I am to be gathered unto my people: bury me with my fathers in the cave that *is* in the field of Ephron the Hittite, ³⁰ In the cave that *is* in the field of Machpelah, which *is* before Mamre, in the land of Canaan, which Abraham bought with the field of Ephron the Hittite for a possession of a buryingplace. ³¹ There they buried Abraham and Sarah his wife; there they buried Isaac and Rebekah his wife; and there I buried Leah. ³² The purchase of the field and of the cave that *is* therein *was* from the children of Heth. ³³ And when Jacob had made an end of commanding his sons, he gathered up his feet into the bed, and yielded up the ghost, and was gathered unto his people. Gen 49:1-33

In the first verse of Genesis 49, Jacob reveals that he would tell them what would befall them "in <u>the Last Days</u>." Note the use of the definite article "the" in Jacob's words. This becomes important because it is proof that Jacob is not discussing their individual "ends" as individuals. Rather he is speaking in a prophetic way. As he passes along the blessings to his heirs, he is uniquely qualified to pass on to the next generation a prophetic word because on the nature of the covenant which God had made to his grandfather Abraham. The unconditional nature of the covenant under-girds the confidence Jacob as he passes along the blessings to another generation. From Jacob's perspective, many aspects of the covenant had not yet been realized, and would not be realized for many centuries. Delays in the full realization of the covenant were inevitable, however the outcome was certain. All this based on the unconditional promises of God made to Abraham in Genesis 22:15-18 which are future in tense.

For the first time, there was a large family of sons (twelve) to divide the birthright and the spiritual blessings. These must now be passed on to future generations. Previously, God chose to place both blessings in the possession of one of just two sons of the generation. Isaac and Jacob had each been chosen over Ishmael and Esau in their respective generation. Now, under the leadership of God, Jacob divides the spiritual blessing and the material blessing. The result is that the spiritual blessing is in the possession of one line and the material blessing of another within the lineage of Israel. A fundamental change in the way God has chosen to transfer the covenant blessings from generation to generation.

The Birthright passed to Joseph in its entirety. The choice of Joseph by Jacob to carry on the lineage of birthright is not out of line, even though Joseph had older brothers. Joseph was the first born of Jacob's wife of God's choosing, Rachael (Genesis 30:22-23). In this single action by Jacob, the Spiritual or Scepter Line is placed in the lineage of Judah while the Birthright or Material Line is in the lineage of Joseph. Only God knows why Jacob was to pass along his blessings in such a way. Nonetheless, it is the line of Judah that Jesus would be born into; ushering in salvation to all men.

The remaining ten sons of Jacob were completely excluded from the enormous plan God had for Judah and Joseph to carryout to their lineages. However, they would be able to participate in both the blessings in ways that are more indirect. Not the least of which would be the blessing of salvation through Jesus Christ.

Now fast forward some five centuries of Israelite history. The tribes of Israel have spent 430 years in Egyptian slavery and another 40 years of wilderness wandering. Moses is about to die and pass the torch of leadership to Joshua. However, before he dies, he blesses the children of Israel in the name of God (see Deuteronomy 33). The twelve sons of Israel have long been dead, but the tribes remained intact. Each had maintained its own individual identity throughout the long years of slavery and wandering. It is interesting to note here that as Moses pronounces the blessings that it is limited and actually absent for some tribes. He specifically blesses Judah (Scepter Line) and Levi (priesthood line), but others only generally.

However, when he comes to the Tribe of Joseph, he confirmed and expanded with further detail the material blessings given to Ephraim and Manasseh. The words of Moses indicate that the blessings will be worldwide, to be poured out upon all mankind through them.

> And of Joseph he said, Blessed of the LORD *be* his land, for the precious things of heaven, for the dew, and for the deep that coucheth beneath, ¹⁴ And for the precious fruits *brought forth* by the sun, and for the precious things put forth by the moon,
>
> ¹⁵ And for the chief things of the ancient mountains, and for the precious things of the lasting hills, ¹⁶ And for the precious things of the earth and fulness thereof, and *for* the good will of him that dwelt in the bush: let *the blessing* come upon the head of Joseph, and upon the top of the head of him *that was* separated from his brethren. ¹⁷ His glory *is like* the firstling of his bullock, and his horns *are like* the horns of unicorns: with them he shall push the people together to the ends of the earth: and they *are* the ten thousands of Ephraim, and they *are* the thousands of Manasseh. Deut 33:13-17

Is there any doubt that God has a special blessing and a task for the tribes of Joseph; and that this blessing is to be carried out through his sons lineage, that of Ephraim and Manasseh? To make it very plain, below is a list reviewing the blessings God made through Moses in these five verses. The prelude to this list Moses says, "Blessed of the Lord be his land," then the list follows.

- *for the precious things of heaven,*
- *for the dew, and for the deep*

- *for the precious fruits brought forth by the sun,*
- *for the precious things put forth by the moon*
- *for the chief things of the ancient mountains,*
- *for the precious things of the lasting hills,*
- *for the precious things of the earth and fullness thereof,*
- *let the blessing come upon the head of Joseph,*
- *His glory is like the firstling of his bullock,*
- *his horns are like the horns of unicorns*
- *he shall push the people together to the ends of the earth*
- *they are* the ten thousands of Ephraim,
- and they are the thousands of Manasseh.

Within this list is found a confirmation of the joint blessings manifested through Joseph's sons. The younger son, Ephraim, received the greater portion of the blessing revealed here as being ten times that of his older brother. This concept should sound familiar. In Genesis 48:19 Jacob blessed the two sons of Joseph with these words, "he (Manasseh) also shall become a people, and he also shall be great: but truly his younger brother shall be greater than he, and his seed shall become a multitude of nations." The historical record validates the accuracy of God's Word in prophecy becoming reality. Some 470 years before Moses speaks these words, God had revealed to Jacob that the inheritance of the younger would be greater than that of the older.

The nature of these blessings listed is all material. Among these blessings, nothing is said about grace, salvation, or anything spiritual. These promises all deal with wealth, riches, land, worldwide expansion, and the abundance from God's created world. It is a very impressive list. But, when added to the previous promises God gave Abraham and subsequent generations up to Joseph that deal primarily with material blessings, the list leaves little to the imagination. The scope and magnitude entailed in these blessings include:

To Abraham God said…

- I will make thee a great nation – Gen. 12:2
- I will bless them that bless thee and curse them that curse thee – Gen 12:3
- I will make they seed as the dust of the earth – Gen 13:16
- I am thy shield and great reward – Gen. 15:1
- I will make nations of thee and Kings shall come out of thee – Gen 17:7
- Thy seed shall possess the gate of his enemies - Gen. 22:17

Of Sarah he said…

- She shall be a mother of nations
- Kings of peoples shall be of her

After Abraham passed these blessings to Isaac, he sent him along with his servant under oath and the divine guidance of God. They were guided directly to Rebekah. In spite of the subterfuge and delay on the part of Laban, God had led Isaac to his chosen wife. Through Laban God would say that she would be, "the mother of thousands of millions, and let thy seed possess the gate of those which hate them." (Gen. 24:60) God thus also uses Rebekah, as he had Sarah earlier, to add to the list of material blessings bestowed upon this family.

Previously referenced was the next generation of Isaac's sons, Esau and Jacob. In these two, Isaac had the opportunity to divide the spiritual and material blessings.

It seemed for a while that this would be the natural course of events to come, but it was not to be so. God intervened when Rebekah finally conceived.

> And the Lord said to her: Two nations are in your womb; people will [come] from you and be separated. One people will be stronger than the other, the older will serve the younger Gen 25:23 (HCSB)

God's prophetic words to Rebekah presented a very accurate picture of what was to come. Esau, the oldest, was generally set aside and Jacob took center stage. Through his own deceit, and with the help of his mother, Jacob received both the birthright and the blessing of Isaac. The events of Jacobs's twelve sons have been covered in detail. As shown in Gen. 49, the birthright/material blessings went to Joseph with the scepter/spiritual blessings going to Judah.

Fast Forwarding Once Again

In history four hundred years from Moses through Joshua's conquest and the subsequent occupation of the Promised Land; Through the Judges, the Kings, Saul, David, Solomon and up to Solomon's wicked son Rehoboam there were wars and conflict. Through this entire period of history, not much is said about the tribes of Ephraim and Manasseh. Only their occupation of the land and their participation in some battles in which they were victorious. However, with the emergence of Jeroboam[7] in

---

[7] Note To Remember: Rehoboam was of the Tribe of Judah, The Scepter Line; Jeroboam was of the Tribe of Ephraim – The Birthright Line

the Biblical record, their presence is again seen. A major part of Prophecy is beginning to be fulfilled.

> ⁴³And Solomon slept with his fathers, and was buried in the city of David his father: and Rehoboam his son reigned in his stead. ¹ And Rehoboam went to Shechem: for all Israel were come to Shechem to make him king. ² And it came to pass, when Jeroboam the son of Nebat, who was yet in Egypt, heard *of it*, (for he was fled from the presence of king Solomon, and Jeroboam dwelt in Egypt;)   1 Kings 11:- 12:2

The following verses tell that the people called Jeroboam out of Egypt and the entire congregation went with Jeroboam to Rehoboam for a conference. Jeroboam attempted to negotiate improved living conditions for the people of Israel. Their pleadings were to no avail as Rehoboam rejected the proposals and threatened them with higher taxes and more strenuous living conditions. (v. 3 & 4) Who was this man Jeroboam? The man in the "ragged coat" torn into twelve pieces by the prophet Ahijah the Shilonite (1 Kings 11:29). Chapter 11 gives us some amazing information about Jeroboam.

- He once was Solomon's servant – v. 26
- He had lifted up his hand (rebelled) against Solomon – v. 26
- He was a mighty man of valor – v. 28
- He was in charge of the house of Joseph – v. 28
- He was an Ephrathite (that is he was of the Tribe of Ephraim) – v. 26

There seems to be a pattern here and God's plans and promises are once more beginning to become more obvious. The most profound qualification Jeroboam possessed when he spoke to Rehoboam (the supposed new king of Israel in chapter 12) was based in an event that took place at the time he left Jerusalem. At that time, he (Jeroboam) had already been given the Kingdom of Israel upon the death of Solomon. Amazing, as it may seem, the Kingdom of Israel was no longer to remain in the linage of David and had not been given to Rehoboam; only the scepter line was to remain under his leadership. Israel as a nation was to be separated from the Nation of Judah, not to be reunited until the second coming of Christ (see Ezekiel 37:15-22 for confirmation). Two nations emerge, one composed of ten tribes, and the other composed of two tribes. Beginning in 1 Kings 11:29, look at this amazing truth.

The Man in the Ragged Coat

²⁹ And it came to pass at that time when Jeroboam went out of Jerusalem, that the prophet Ahijah the Shilonite found him in the way; and he had clad himself with a new garment; and they two *were* alone in the field: ³⁰ And Ahijah caught the new garment that *was* on him, and rent it *in* twelve pieces: ³¹ And he said to Jeroboam, Take thee ten pieces: for thus saith the LORD, the God of Israel, Behold, I will rend the kingdom out of the hand of Solomon, and will give ten tribes to thee: ³² (But he shall have one tribe for my servant David's sake, and for Jerusalem's sake, the city which I have chosen out of all the tribes of Israel:)

³³ Because that they have forsaken me, and have worshipped Ashtoreth the goddess of the Zidonians, Chemosh the god of the Moabites, and Milcom the god of the children of Ammon, and have not walked in my ways, to do *that which is* right in mine eyes, and *to keep* my statutes and my judgments, as *did* David his father. ³⁴ Howbeit I will not take the whole kingdom out of his hand: but I will make him prince all the days of his life for David my servant's sake, whom I chose, because he kept my commandments and my statutes:

³⁵ But I will take the kingdom out of his son's hand, and will give it unto thee, *even* ten tribes. ³⁶ And unto his son will I give one tribe, that David my servant may have a light alway before me in Jerusalem, the city which I have chosen me to put my name there. ³⁷ And I will take thee, and thou shalt reign according to all that thy soul desireth, and shalt be king over Israel. ³⁸ And it shall be, if thou wilt hearken unto all that I command thee, and wilt walk in my ways, and do *that is* right in my sight, to keep my statutes and my commandments, as David my servant did; that I will be with thee, and build thee a sure house, as I built for David, and will give Israel unto thee. ³⁹ And I will for this afflict the seed of David, but not for ever. ⁴⁰ Solomon sought therefore to kill Jeroboam. And Jeroboam arose, and fled into Egypt, unto Shishak king of Egypt, and was in Egypt until the death of Solomon.   1 Kings 11:29-40

At the time Rehoboam, son of Solomon, declared himself king, **Israel already had a King, Jeroboam.** Ahijah, the prophet of God, had already anointed Jeroboam. Therefore, only the Tribe of Judah remained under the leadership of Rehoboam. His kingship of Judah was not because of his leadership skills but a direct result of the promise God had made to his grandfather David years before.

To Your Tents, O Israel

In the 12th chapter of I Kings, several events take place that affected the entire world for centuries to come.

- Jeroboam, the rightful king of Israel (not Judah), unsuccessfully tried to make peace with Rehoboam and unify Israel and Judah – v. 3-17
- Rehoboam sent Adoram, the tax collector. to Israel and he was stoned – v. 16
- Israel rebelled against the House of David (Judah) – v: 19
- Rehoboam assembled all of Judah and some of Benjamin to fight against Israel in order to reunite the kingdom again under his rule – v. 21
- God took control and sent one of his prophets, Shemaiah, to Rehoboam advising him not to go up and fight against his brethren, the children of Israel proclaiming "this thing is from me." V 23-24

It was now time for God to intervene once again. This time God set up conditions whereby all the promises that had unconditionally been made to their forefathers could now be carried out. One more event was taking place so the Scepter Line could be established in Judah. Both nations were about to embark on centuries of sin and rebellion. This national sin did not negate the promises of

God. It did however result in the delay of the fulfillment of God's promises to the children of Israel.

Jeroboam built Schechem in Mount Ephraim and later built Penuel. Moving further north, he established his capitol at Samaria. Worse, he implemented several religious practices that would seem to be blasphemous enough to exclude the Nation of Israel from receiving any of God's blessings. God would not allow such to be the case. Remember that he had declared through his prophet, "this thing is from me[8]."

> [25] Then Jeroboam built Shechem in mount Ephraim, and dwelt therein; and went out from thence, and built Penuel. [26] And Jeroboam said in his heart, Now shall the kingdom return to the house of David: [27] If this people go up to do sacrifice in the house of the LORD at Jerusalem, then shall the heart of this people turn again unto their Lord, *even* unto Rehoboam king of Judah, and they shall kill me, and go again to Rehoboam king of Judah. [28] Whereupon the king took counsel, and made two calves *of* gold, and said unto them, It is too much for you to go up to Jerusalem: behold thy gods, O Israel, which brought thee up out of the land of Egypt. [29] And he set the one in Bethel, and the other put he in Dan. [30] And this thing became a sin: for the people went *to worship* before the one, *even* unto Dan. [31] And he made an house of high places, and made priests of the lowest of the people, which were not of the sons of Levi. [32] And Jeroboam ordained a feast in the eighth month, on the fifteenth day of the month, like unto the feast that *is* in Judah, and he offered upon the altar. So did he in Bethel, sacrificing unto the calves that he had made: and he placed in Bethel the priests of the high places which he had made. [33] So he offered upon the altar which he had made in Bethel the fifteenth day of the eighth month, *even* in the month which he had devised of his own heart; and ordained a feast unto the children of Israel: and he offered upon the altar, and burnt incense. 1 Kings 12:25-33

---

[8] I Kings 12:24

These verses give us insight into Jeroboam's implementation of his idea of reform for the Northern Kingdom. Looking at Jeroboam, he appears to be an unlikely choice for God to use to develop the birthright blessings. The pivotal verse to remember is 12:24, "this thing is of me." Jeroboam's attempt to reform the people is no surprise to God. Throughout history God used, and continues to use surprising events to fulfill his covenant promises. In three major events, God used persecution to develop his people, Israel, into a nation that would carry out His planned blessing.

(1) Consider the Exodus. For four hundred and thirty years, God used the persecution of Egypt to develop Jacob's rag-tag seventy families into a multitude of four million people.
(2) Then, for forty years of desert wanderings, God developed the multitude of disorganized complainers, (and the people complained against Moses, Ex. 15:24) into a new nation ready to start God's plan.
(3) This same pattern of persecution to develop God's people into a people of blessing is repeated in the New Testament. In Acts 2, God again allowed the persecution by Jewish and Roman leaders to change 120 new believers into a band of individuals devoted to spreading the Gospel of Christ to the entire world. This unlikely group emerged from the twelve to the one hundred and twenty to a new people defined by their faith. A people of a New Covenant called to carry out the spiritual (scepter) blessings promised so long ago.

The accounts in I Kings show the rejection of the law of God through the leadership of Jeroboam. By sponsoring an unqualified priest, Jeroboam leads Israel to reject the Priestly line of Levi. Additionally, he changed the feast days God had ordained. Worst of all, he changed God's law of the seventh-day-Sabbath to an eighth-day-Sabbath, a pagan practice of worship. (Sunday) Instead of honoring God, who had given him the ten tribes known as Israel, he set them up for a great fall. An important point to make here is that God, through his prophet Abijah, declared that he would give Rehoboam (son of Solomon) one tribe. "...*will give one tribe to thy son for David my servant's sake, and for Jerusalem's sake which I have chosen."* (1 Kings 11:13)

A Sad Beginning

From the decision of Jeroboam through the next nineteen kings, approximately 260 years, the new Nation of Israel rejected God and his laws. A few righteous kings who tried to restore true worship of God briefly interrupted this falling away. Their efforts, however, were very limited in scope and mostly unsuccessful and short lived. "Ephraim is joined to idols, let him alone," said God through his prophet Hosea. (Hosea 4:17) Concerning the priests set up by Jeroboam, Hosea labeled them "a snare" (5:1) to the people.

PAYDAY SOMEDAY

For two and a half centuries, the two kingdoms remained divided. Then God allowed the Kingdom of Assyria to bring to a temporary end the Kingdom of Israel, as recorded in 2 Kings 17.

> ¹ In the twelfth year of Ahaz king of Judah began Hoshea the son of Elah to reign in Samaria over Israel nine years. ² And he did *that which was* evil in the sight of the LORD, but not as the kings of Israel that were before him. ³ Against him came up Shalmaneser king of Assyria; and Hoshea became his servant, and gave him presents. ⁴ And the king of Assyria found conspiracy in Hoshea: for he had sent messengers to So king of Egypt, and brought no present to the king of Assyria, as *he had done* year by year: therefore the king of Assyria shut him up, and bound him in prison.
>
> ⁵ Then the king of Assyria came up throughout all the land, and went up to Samaria, and besieged it three years. ⁶ In the ninth year of Hoshea the king of Assyria took Samaria, and carried Israel away into Assyria, and placed them in Halah and in Habor *by* the river of Gozan, and in the cities of the Medes.
>
> ⁷ For *so* it was, that the children of Israel had sinned against the LORD their God, which had brought them up out of the land of Egypt, from under the hand of Pharaoh king of Egypt, and had feared other gods, ⁸ And walked in the statutes of the heathen, whom the LORD cast out from before the children of Israel, and of the kings of Israel, which they had made. ⁹ And the children of Israel did secretly *those* things that *were* not right against the LORD their God, and they built them high places in all their cities, from the tower of the watchmen to the fenced city. ¹⁰ And they set them up images and groves in every high hill, and under every green tree: ¹¹ And there they burnt incense in all the high places, as *did* the heathen whom the LORD carried away before them; and wrought wicked things to provoke the LORD to anger: ¹² For they served idols, whereof the LORD had said unto them, Ye shall not do this thing. ¹³ Yet the LORD testified against Israel, and against Judah, by all the

prophets, *and by* all the seers, saying, Turn ye from your evil ways, and keep my commandments *and* my statutes, according to all the law which I commanded your fathers, and which I sent to you by my servants the prophets. **14** Notwithstanding they would not hear, but hardened their necks, like to the neck of their fathers, that did not believe in the LORD their God. **15** And they rejected his statutes, and his covenant that he made with their fathers, and his testimonies which he testified against them; and they followed vanity, and became vain, and went after the heathen that *were* round about them, *concerning* whom the LORD had charged them, that they should not do like them. **16** And they left all the commandments of the LORD their God, and made them molten images, *even* two calves, and made a grove, and worshipped all the host of heaven, and served Baal. **17** And they caused their sons and their daughters to pass through the fire, and used divination and enchantments, and sold themselves to do evil in the sight of the LORD, to provoke him to anger. **18** Therefore the LORD was very angry with Israel, and removed them out of his sight: there was none left but the Tribe of Judah only. **19** Also Judah kept not the commandments of the LORD their God, but walked in the statutes of Israel which they made. **20** And the LORD rejected all the seed of Israel, and afflicted them, and delivered them into the hand of spoilers, until he had cast them out of his sight. **21** For he rent Israel from the house of David; and they made Jeroboam the son of Nebat king: and Jeroboam drave Israel from following the LORD, and made them sin a great sin. **22** For the children of Israel walked in all the sins of Jeroboam which he did; they departed not from them; **23** Until the LORD removed Israel out of his sight, as he had said by all his servants the prophets. So was Israel carried away out of their own land to Assyria unto this day. 2 Kings 17

Thus, the Nation of Israel was taken captive, becoming slaves to the King of Assyria. An event, which appeared to be the end of the Kingdoms of Israel, actually becomes just another step in the plan of God. In spite of Israel's rejection and apparent demise, God still intends to be faithful to all the promises of the birthright made to that nation. From this point in history, they never will return to the land of their fathers until the re-gathering of both kingdoms. This reunion comes about at the close of The Age. Scripture makes clear this plan in many Old Testament and New Testament passages. Take for example the words of Isaiah 11:10-18 and Ezekiel 37:15-20. Both scriptures foretell the unifying of the two nations into one in the Last Days. Many other Prophets foretell the same unifying of the two Nations. (See later chapters)

> [10] And in that day there shall be a root of Jesse, which shall stand for an ensign of the people; to it shall the Gentiles seek: and his rest shall be glorious. [11] And it shall come to pass in that day, *that* the Lord shall set his hand again the second time to recover the remnant of his people, which shall be left, from Assyria, and from Egypt, and from Pathros, and from Cush, and from Elam, and from Shinar, and from Hamath, and from the islands of the sea.

> [12] And he shall set up an ensign for the nations, and shall assemble the outcasts of Israel, and gather together the dispersed of Judah from the four corners of the earth. [13] The envy also of Ephraim shall depart, and the adversaries of Judah shall be cut off: Ephraim shall not envy Judah, and Judah shall not vex Ephraim Isaiah 11:10-13

> [15] The word of the LORD came again unto me, saying, [16] Moreover, thou son of man, take thee one stick, and write upon it, For Judah, and for the children of Israel his companions: then take another stick, and write upon it, For Joseph, the stick of Ephraim, and *for* all the house of Israel his companions: [17] And join them one to another into one stick; and they shall become one in thine hand. [18] And when the children of thy people shall speak unto thee, saying, Wilt thou not shew us what thou *meanest* by these? [19] Say unto them, Thus saith the Lord GOD; Behold, I will take the stick of Joseph, which *is* in the hand of Ephraim, and the tribes of Israel his fellows, and will put them with him, *even* with the stick of Judah, and make them one stick, and they shall be one in mine hand.

> [20] And the sticks whereon thou writest shall be in thine hand before their eyes. [21] And say unto them, Thus saith the Lord GOD; Behold, I will take the children of Israel from among the heathen, whither they be gone, and will gather them on every side, and bring them into their own land: [22] And I will make them one nation in the land upon the mountains of Israel; and one king shall be king to them all: and they shall be no more two nations, neither shall they be divided into two kingdoms any more at all: Ezek 37:15-22

Clearly, these passages point to a future restoration of the two kingdoms in a unified national identity. The apostle Paul speaks of this same re-gathering in Romans 11:26. *"And so all Israel shall be saved: as it is written, There shall come out of Sion the Deliverer, and shall turn away ungodliness from Jacob."* (Romans 11:26) The tense of Paul's writing is future, indicating that the salvation of all Israel has not yet happened. Since Paul is writing after the death of Christ, salvation is to come to all Israel at a future time. Along with these, many prophets of the Old Testament include passages indicating a future reunification of the two kingdoms. Elijah, Elisha, Hosea, Amos, Isaiah, Micah, and Jeremiah all spoke about this eventuality. Calling for repentance of their sin they prophesized to both Judah and Israel, warning how God would punish them as kingdoms. Their pleas were to no avail. The people of both kingdoms pursued other gods and both received their separate punishments. The Kingdom of Israel lasted only two hundred and fifty years (B.C. 975-721) and Judah only three hundred and eighty-nine years (BC 977-588). While Israel and Judah suffered from the postponement of realizing God's blessings, God is not finished with them. Leviticus 26 outlines a time frame for God's blessings being withheld (twenty eight times), and Ezekiel and Genesis confirm and clarify this truth (later explained).

BLESSINGS DENIED – BLESSINGS DELAYED

In order to understand the withholding of God's promised blessing for a definite period of time, consider evidence in the book of Exodus. When Moses led the children of Israel out of bondage in Egypt, God began an active and daily guiding process over them. In Exodus 12 at the institution of the Passover, God spoke and said, *"This month shall be unto you the beginning of months: it shall be the first month of the year to you."* (Ex 12:2) God established a calendar for his people, beginning that very day. In this "Happy New Year" from God, he went on to establish the worship and feast days for Israel. God then commanded that this calendar be forever. *"And ye shall observe this thing for an ordinance to thee and to thy sons for ever."* (Ex 12:24)

Following this, for over two month's God lead them in their escape from Egypt as they moved toward the Red Sea. *"And the LORD went before them by day in a pillar of a cloud, to lead them the way; and by night in a pillar of fire, to give them light; to go by day and night."* (Ex 13:21) Not only did he lead them, he also provided food in the form of manna, quail, and pure water. In so doing, God began to re-establish the Sabbath Day of worship (Ex. 16:23 & 29). These provisions continued for forty years, until Israel came to the border of the Land of Canaan (v. 35).

"In the third month, when the children of Israel were gone forth out of the land of Egypt, the same day came they into the wilderness of Sinai." (Ex 19:1) A more detailed summary account of their journey up to the point of moving into the Promised Land is given in Numbers 33. As they camp at the foot of Mount Sinai, God declares his blessings if Israel will keep his commandments.

> [5] Now therefore, if ye will obey my voice indeed, and keep my covenant, then ye shall be a peculiar treasure unto me above all people: for all the earth *is* mine: [6] And ye shall be unto me a kingdom of priests, and an holy nation. These *are* the words which thou shalt speak unto the children of Israel.
>
> [7] And Moses came and called for the elders of the people, and laid before their faces all these words which the LORD commanded him. [8] And all the people answered together, and said, <u>All that the LORD hath spoken we will do</u>. And Moses returned the words of the people unto the LORD. Ex 19:5-8

In short, the people reply to Moses with a resounding, "yes Lord, sounds like a good deal to us, and of course we will do anything you say!" Like most *deals with God*, once they knew God would bless them, they forgot about their agreement to keep the Covenant. In fact, before Moses returned from his second trip to the Holy Mountain, they had already turned from God's law. However, within these four verses of scripture cited above are several important promises.

- You shall be a peculiar treasure above all people
- You will be a Kingdom of priests
- A holy nation

While God makes a number of unconditional promises or covenants with his people, this is not one of them. These promises are conditional[9] upon the people of Israel

---

[9] This conditional covenant is in contrast to the covenant of Genesis 22.16-18 and extended upon elsewhere. This unconditional covenant establishes the national and spiritual blessings promised through Abraham. The Abraham covenant pertains to the birthright and blessing lines. Taking care to "rightly divide the word," these two covenants in no way conflict with one another.

obeying God in two particular ways. They were to obey his voice and keep his commandments. These conditions must be met for the blessings to be received.

Additionally, the "peculiar treasure" referred to here is later described in Amos. *"For, lo, I will command, and I will sift the house of Israel among all nations, like as corn is sifted in a sieve, yet shall not the least grain fall upon the earth."* (Amos 9:9) All Israel will know the promise of God. They will be dispersed, but never forgotten by God in his plan of salvation. As Paul declares, *"And so all Israel shall be saved: as it is written, There shall come out of Sion the Deliverer, and shall turn away ungodliness from Jacob."* (Romans 11:26) Furthermore, Jesus gave insight regarding God's treasures. Matthew records Jesus' teaching about the Kingdom of heaven in parable form. *"Again, the Kingdom of heaven is like unto treasure hid in a field; the which when a man hath found, he hideth, and for joy thereof goeth and selleth all that he hath, and buyeth that field."* (Matt 13:44) Taken by itself, this passage seems to have little to do with the Old Testament covenants. However, this scripture is not to be taken by itself. Each passage is a part of a whole, a part of the passages surrounding it. The wording of this passage is defined in the immediately preceding passages. For instance in verse 37, Jesus identifies the "man" as the Son of God. In verse 38, he identifies the "field" as the "world." With this in mind, the parable can be understood as, "God gave all he had (his son) to purchase (save) the field (world, where his treasure Israel is hidden or sifted)." In Christ, those who overcome are promised;

- Power over the nations – Rev. 2:26
- Rule the nations with a rod of Iron – 2:27
- Be a pillar in the temple of God – 3:12
- God's name will be on them – 3:12
- New Jerusalem, God's City will be named – 3:12
- Will sit upon the throne with Jesus – 3:21

This overcoming is accomplished thru God's grace and the leadership of the Holy Spirit. Here, we have digressed a bit to show that God is moving his people thru history in a manner in which there is punishment for sin, but sin does not negate God's promises and purposes.

Returning to Exodus 32, consider the time which Israel actually trusts God's leadership and obey his commandments. At the foot of the mountain, awaiting Moses' return from the presence of God, quickly they fall into idolatrous worship. So complete was this idolatrous movement within the camp that even Moses' brother, Aaron was not immune. God's anger nearly erupted into destruction of the whole of the people. A testament to the power of prayer is seen through Moses' intervention and pleading to God on behalf of the people. It was the remembrance of the sacred promise of God to Abraham, Isaac, and Israel (Jacob) that averted destruction. These promises are so powerful because of their unconditional nature. Upon being reminded of them by Moses, God repented (changed his mind), of "the evil, which he thought to do to his people." (Ex. 32:14) It is important to note that Israel was only three days journey away from the promised land (Canaan). As the people draw close to realizing this part of God's promise, He gives Moses instructions that are intended to keep this people a holy nation. He is given the Law, the pattern for the tabernacle and its altar, and all the direction needed to live under His protection. The result would be a people who would know first hand the full extent of both God's protection and his blessings. In the books of Leviticus and Numbers we find detailed instructions, warnings and promises that resulted from God's meeting Moses on the mountain.

YEAR FOR A DAY

In this section, we examine some key scriptures showing how God keeps his promises and covenants, even to a sinful nation, a nation loved dearly, despite their rebellious tendencies. In Numbers 13, God fully instructed and prepared his people for the occupation of the Land of Promise.

> [1] The LORD spoke to Moses: [2] "Send men to scout out the land of Canaan I am giving to the Israelites. Send one man who is a leader among them from each of their ancestral tribes." [3] Moses sent them from the Wilderness of Paran at the LORD's command. All the men were leaders in Israel. Num 13:1-3 (HCSB)

Following these instructions, a list of twelve men, one from each tribe, are sent as spies into the land of Canaan. In verses 17 through 20, Moses gives them final instructions. Moving through the land during a time of harvest, they are to determine both the quality of the land and the strength of the inhabitants. The expedition has become a familiar story. The tale they tell upon their return confirms God's promise of a land of milk and honey. The blessings of plentiful harvests must have given the people an immediate sense of excitement. Then the disappointment hit. The report of the ten echoed the fear that had resulted from their forty-day spy mission. The harvest was great, but the walled cities inhabited by giant warriors caused the ten to conclude that the people of God could not prevail.

The majority report of the ten following forty days (Num. 13:25), was the absolute worse the children of Israel could imagine. Without regard to how God had provided for the people of the Exodus thus far, the ten were swayed by the fierce appearance of the people they encountered.

Their walled cities seemed equally unconquerable. Only Joshua (Tribe of Ephraim) and Caleb (Tribe of Judah) looked through the eyes of faith. They believed that with the help of God, the people would indeed prevail to claim the fullness of God's promise. As people often do, the children of Israel chose to believe what they could not do instead of what God could do. Therefore, the people heard the report of the ten, they wept, cried, and called for a new leader to take the place of Moses and lead them back to slavery in Egypt. Once more God's people failed to trust him and the truth of his promises. Nothing Joshua, Caleb, or Moses could say would sway them to accept and claim that which God had promised would be theirs.

Imagine God's disappointment as he saw the faint heartedness of his children. Instead of victory, the Israelites find themselves on the wrong side of God's Word. God's decision - all adult Israelites living at the end of that day would wander in the wilderness until they all die. All except the two who believed, Joshua and Caleb. It would become the task of the children to survive the years of wilderness wandering and occupy the land. These God judged innocent, determining they had no part in the nation's unbelief. The length of this sentence is explained in Numbers 14:26-39, with verse 34 being key. *After the number of the days in which ye searched the land, even forty days, each day for a year, shall ye bear your iniquities, even forty years, and ye shall know my breach of promise.*

It is in this context in which God set up a period of punishment often referred to as "a day for a year" or "a year for a day." This same time equivalency principle is used at other times in prophecy, especially in the realm of delayed blessings and punishment. Here God imposed a year's punishment for each day the spies searched the land, saw God's bounty, and did not trust Him enough to report back favorably to the people. Because of their lack of faith, the people of God would not cross over the Jordan River and occupy the land.

This is an important principle to see in use by God. God will impose it again, and again, upon the people of Israel in response to their sin. The judgment and corresponding punishment by God is not his final verdict, however. In spite of the failure and sin of the people, His unconditional promise regarding the birthright nations (tribes) continues.

BLESSINGS DELAYED AGAIN

In the preceding chapter, God uses a system to reveal time through prophecy, which can be proven by applying historical events, thus confirming its accuracy. Using the lunar year of 360 days for a year and 30 days for a month, the historical accuracy is proven. Most importantly, we have shown that God uses the principle "of a year for a day" and "a day a year" in scripture. Furthermore, it is absolutely imperative that we allow scripture to interpret itself, not imposing a personal idea on scripture. Simply allowing historical facts and events to confirm scriptural prophecy, they confirm this principle.

With this principle firmly in place, we return to the central truth of this section, when and where the Birthright Promises were fulfilled in Israel.

1. Joseph was the birthright Line (nation) through Joseph and his sons. See Genesis 48-49, 1 Chronicles 5:1-2
2. Judah was the scepter line (nation) from which Christ would come. See Genesis 48-49
3. The Nation of Israel separated from Judah in approximately 980 BC after rejecting Yahweh as their true God, and immediately set up false gods in Samaria.[10] 1 Kings 12
4. For approximately 260 years the nation Israel lived in Samaria worshipping false gods, completely

---

[10] Note: Remember when referring to the nations of Israel and Judah, the Northern and Southern Kingdoms are implied. Israel consisted of ten tribes. Judah consisted of two tribes plus remnants of Levi.

abandoning God's laws and commandments. In 721 BC God permitted the Assyrians to conquer Israel. Subsequently, Israel was taken into captivity and later scattered without receiving God's promised birthright blessing as a result of their sin. *For the children of Israel walked in all the sins of Jeroboam which he did; they departed not from them;* ²³ *Until the LORD removed Israel out of his sight, as he had said by all his servants the prophets. So was Israel carried away out of their own land to Assyria unto this day.* 2 Kings 17:22-23

Remember that God had already given a period of 390 years using the principle of a "day for a year" to identify Israel's sin and subsequent delayed blessing (Ezekiel 4). This period of time lasts from 1111 BC (1 Samuel 8 rejection of God's rule) until 721 BC (God casts them from his site in 2 Kings 17). God warned of such a judgment at various places in scripture including his instructions through Moses in Leviticus.

The Real Meat of God's Prophecy to Israel

In Leviticus 25:55, following an extensive listing of laws and instructions, God proclaims, *For unto me the children of Israel are servants; they are my servants whom I brought forth out of the land of Egypt: I am the LORD your God.* Lev 25:55 Then, God gives through Moses one of the most detailed instructions and warnings in all of scripture to Israel summarized here in Lev.26:33, *And I will scatter you among the heathen, and will draw out a sword after you: and your land shall be desolate, and your cities waste.* Lev 26:33 It is also one of the most difficult prophetic time-line passages to understand. Unless the principle of "a day for a year" is applied, it is nearly impossible to understand God's delay or withholding of his blessings. Numbers 13 and Ezekiel again must be kept in mind to establish the principle (both scriptures previously detailed).

Looking Back – Apples for Apples

In the twenty-first century, we have a perfectly legitimate and scripturally valid method of understanding prophecy after the prophesized event takes place. Lets review for clarification.

1. Revelation 13 – the deadly wound is healed and the beast (Roman Empire) was allowed to continue for forty and two months = 1260 days
2. Using the principle of "day for a year" and "year for a day" the deadly wound is healed by Justinian in 554 AD
3. This healing continued until the complete demise of the Empire in 1814 AD
4. Thus 1260 days = 1260 years; 1814 – 554 = 1260[11]

These historical dates are repeated here in conjunction with the Biblical years and dates for emphasis. They are strong validating events to confirm the principle used to interpret and understand prophecy. The unconditional promises God made to Abraham, Isaac, Jacob and his sons Ephraim and Manasseh can now be considered by taking a look at history. Have the unconditional promises, which are prophecy, concerning the material blessings been fulfilled. Has A nation and a company of nations, as outlined in Genesis 48:15-20, experienced this pouring out of God's blessings. If so, when did God bring world events together to accomplish this?

---

[11] For more information, see West,. The Holy Roman Empire. [Electronic Version]

Beginning in the 1700's, relatively small, growing nations among much larger world powers began to receive blessing that God had withheld for over 2500 years. During this time, the fledgling United States (consisting of 13 colonies) and the United Kingdom (consisting of the British Isles, Canada, the colony of India, and a few insignificant islands) began to emerge. In the next few years, these two nations burst forth in rapid growth in unprecedented wealth and power. In a very short time period (in historical perspective), the vast list of holdings of the British Empire became quite impressive. In addition to the above nations, this time of British expansion grew to include the continents of Australia and Antarctica, and the British Empire stretching from the British Isles, to Canada, to South Africa, to India, to China along with numerous island nations and smaller colonies. Taken as a whole, they form a commonwealth of nations, unparalleled in history, like that promised to Ephraim in Genesis 48:19.

WHAT'S IN A NAME?

In order to understand the written word, whether secular or scriptural prophesy, here are four good questions to ask yourself.

1. Who said it or wrote it?
2. To whom was it spoken/written?
3. When was it said/written?
4. By what authority was it spoken/written?

For simplicity, we will call these The Four Questions for Understanding. Any search for a solid understanding of scriptural prophecy requires asking these questions. They become safeguards, ensuring the search center on the Word of God and not allow outside thoughts or ideas to influence the result of the search. Using these questions as a guide, consider the following search through scripture to validate the principle of "a day for a year – a year for a day".

Here, we consider Ezekiel 1:1-3.

> ¹ Now it came to pass in the thirtieth year, in the fourth *month*, in the fifth *day* of the month, as I *was* among the captives by the river of Chebar, *that* the heavens were opened, and I saw visions of God. ² In the fifth *day* of the month, which *was* the fifth year of king Jehoiachin's captivity, ³ The word of the LORD came expressly unto Ezekiel the priest, the son of Buzi, in the land of the Chaldeans by the river Chebar; and the hand of the LORD was there upon him. Ezek 1:1-3

Now, continuing in Ezekiel chapter 1, using the Four Questions for Understanding

1. Who wrote it? Ezekiel uses the first person "I" to identify himself as the writer.
2. To whom was it written? Here, we must consider the nature of prophecy. Is his writing intended mainly for his contemporaries, or is it a prophetic writing intended for further generations? Moreover, if to future generations, can we identify to whom it applies? At the time (approximately 600 B.C. – see below), the Kingdom or House of Israel had already gone into Assyrian Captivity in 721 B.C. a full one hundred and twenty years earlier. This would place him in the middle part of the Jewish Captivity, giving him little or no opportunity to preach to the Kingdom of Israel except by prophecy for the future. One method of determining to whom a prophet of God is writing is to look at the terms used to describe God's people in the Old Testament.[12] Over the past hundred years, many prominent writers have used the term "Jew or Jews" when referring to God's people. Such phrases as "the Jews in the wilderness", or "the Jews crossed the Red Sea," or "the Jews crossed over Jordan" are   too common. The lumping of the tribes, nation, house, or people of Israel into one group simply called "The Jews" at this point in history is <u>misleading and false</u>. It damages the understanding of the Word of God. Scripturally, the first use of the term "Jews" is found in 2 Kings 16:6. In this passage, the King of Syria joined with Pedah, <u>King of Israel</u>, in battle against the <u>Jews</u>. This event is also recorded in Isaiah 7:1-9 identifying Ephraim as their leader. The Nation of Juda is identified as the Jews, not all of the tribes,

---

[12] At that time Rezin king of Syria recovered Elath to Syria, and drave the Jews from Elath: and the Syrians came to Elath, and dwelt there unto this day. 2 Kings 16:6

nations, or houses. In scripture, the term "Jew" is used in conjunction with "House of Judah," Nation of Juda, and sometimes called the "Remnant of Israel." In each instance, only the Tribe of Judah along with parts of Benjamin and Levi are identified. The remaining of the ten tribes is identified as "the House of Israel," or the "Nation of Israel." This separation of the ten tribes from Juda and Benjamin is described in 1 Kings 11 and 12. This separation took place at approximately 982 B.C. From that time on, prophecies referring to House of Israel do not include the "Jews." This separation holds until prophecies referring to end times (see Ezekiel 36 – 37), when the House of Judah and the House of Israel are once again united under Christ the King. Prior to the 982 B.C. separation, it was correct to refer to the House of Israel, Children of Israel, and other like terms, which included the Tribe of Judah. The correct understanding, identification and application of these terms, consistent with the Word of God, becomes imperative in order to rightly divide the Word. In Chapter 4, Ezekiel identifies the "whom" as the House of Israel and the House of Judah. They are dealt with individually by God, not as a grouping of "Jews."

3. When was it said or written? Ezekiel identifies the time as "the fifth year of King Jehoiachin's captivity." A well-accepted date of 605 B.C. is the date of the first deportation of the House of Judah. This continued for a period of 18 – 20 years until approximately 587-585 B.C. From other sources, we know that Ezekiel was among the first of the deportees, placing his writing near 600 B.C.

4. By what authority was it written or spoken? Ezekiel 1:3 leaves no doubt that it is under God's authority that Ezekiel is writing. "The word of the LORD came expressly unto Ezekiel the priest, ..."

Understanding the total setting of Ezekiel, using the Four Questions for Understanding, gives us the basis needed to return to the subject of delayed blessings. As previously stated, Ezekiel is in Babylon about five years after the deportation of Judah began and approximately 120 years after Israel ceased to be a nation as a result of the Assyrian Captivity. In Ezekiel 4, God instructs Ezekiel to do two seemingly strange things. One applies to Jerusalem (House of Judah) and the other against the House of Israel. Two distinct and separate acts against two distinct and separate nations for sins they have committed a two different times and places.

> ¹ Thou also, son of man, take thee a tile, and lay it before thee, and pourtray upon it the city, even Jerusalem:
>
> ² And lay siege against it, and build a fort against it, and cast a mount against it; set the camp also against it, and set battering rams against it round about. ³ Moreover take thou unto thee an iron pan, and set it for a wall of iron between thee and the city: and set thy face against it, and it shall be besieged, and thou shalt lay siege against it. This shall be a sign to the house of Israel. ⁴ Lie thou also upon thy left side, and lay the iniquity of the house of Israel upon it: according to the number of the days that thou shalt lie upon it thou shalt bear their iniquity. ⁵ For I have laid upon thee the years of their iniquity, according to the number of the days, three hundred and ninety days: so shalt thou bear the iniquity of the house of Israel.
>
> ⁶ And when thou hast accomplished them, lie again on thy right side, and thou shalt bear the iniquity of the house of Judah forty days: I have appointed thee each day for a year
> Ezek 4:1-17
>
> *Note: Underlining author added for emphasis*

At this point, God is using Ezekiel to warn Israel and Judah, both the Northern and Southern Kingdoms of the divided nation. God is evoking the principle of "a day for a year." Ezekiel could not possibly lay on his side for the

390 years which Israel rejected God plus the 40 years for the sins of Judah. A Day represented a Year instead of a Year representing a Day, as was the case previously in Numbers 13. Chapter 13 of Numbers outlines the events of the Hebrew spies' 40-day mission into the land of Canaan. Their report resulted in a failure to trust God. Not only did they believe conquest of the land to be impossible, their recommendation to the people was to return to Egypt. Chapter 14 culminates with God's Judgment and correlation between the 40-day mission and the 40-year consequences. *After the number of the days in which ye searched the land, even forty days, each day for a year, shall ye bear your iniquities, even forty years, and ye shall know my breach of promise* - Num 14:34

390 Years Against Israel

What does this mean? How does this fit into God's plan to carry out his Birthright Promise to Israel? When did the time of unbelief begin, and when did God decide to end this period of unbelief by withholding the blessings? 1 Samuel gives us the historical information needed to pinpoint this pivotal event when the 390-year rejection began for Israel.

We pick up Samuel's story in Judges. Following the death of Joshua, as recorded in Judges 2:8, Israel's sin is proclaimed.

> [11] And the children of Israel did evil in the sight of the LORD, and served Baalim: [12] And they forsook the LORD God of their fathers, which brought them out of the land of Egypt, and followed other gods, of the gods of the people that *were* round about them, and bowed themselves unto them, and provoked the LORD to anger. [13] And they forsook the LORD, and served Baal and Ashtaroth. [14] And the anger of the LORD was hot against Israel, and he delivered them into the hands of spoilers that spoiled them, and he sold them into the hands of their enemies round about, so

that they could not any longer stand before their enemies. [15] Whithersoever they went out, the hand of the LORD was against them for evil, as the LORD had said, and as the LORD had sworn unto them: and they were greatly distressed. *Judges 2:11-15*

In this passage, it appears that God is bringing rapid punishment for the sins of the people. Such punishment is in keeping with the warnings of God found in Leviticus 26 (this chapter will be addressed later).

However, even in His wrath, the mercy of God was still with Israel. Continuing in Judges 2, this mercy is stated by God.

[16] Nevertheless the LORD raised up judges, which delivered them out of the hand of those that spoiled them. [17] And yet they would not hearken unto their judges, but they went a whoring after other gods, and bowed themselves unto them: they turned quickly out of the way which their fathers walked in, obeying the commandments of the LORD; but they did not so.

[18] And when the LORD raised them up judges, then the LORD was with the judge, and delivered them out of the hand of their enemies all the days of the judge: for it repented the LORD because of their groanings by reason of them that oppressed them and vexed them. [19] And it came to pass, when the judge was dead, that they returned, and corrupted themselves more than their fathers, in following other gods to serve them, and to bow down unto them; they ceased not from their own doings, nor from their stubborn way. *Judges 2:16-19*

The instrument of God's mercy would be the Judges. God took care of a sinning and rebellious nation because of the groaning and intercession of God's selected Judges is an amazing truth. The period of the Judges ended with the death of Samuel. *And it came to pass, when Samuel was old, that he made his sons judges over Israel.* 1 Sam 8:1.

Notice it was Samuel, not God, who appointed Samuel's sons as Judges. Tragedy followed as Samuel assumed this right from God. *And his sons walked not in his ways, but turned aside after lucre, and took bribes, and perverted judgment.* 1 Sam 8:3 . The result could almost be anticipated. Samuel's sons were perverted in their judgment and the people rebelled. *⁴ Then all the elders of Israel gathered themselves together, and came to Samuel unto Ramah, ⁵ And said unto him, Behold, thou art old, and thy sons walk not in thy ways: now make us a king to judge us like all the nations.* 1 Sam 8:4-5.

This is the turning point in God's dealing with his people, Israel. They set in motion a course of events that would show just how far they had drifted from trusting God for their leadership.

1. Samuel appointed his sons as judges
2. These judges were evil and perverted in their judgment
3. The people rebelled against these judges
4. However, instead of confessing their sin and asking God for his guidance, they asked him for a king
5. They wanted to be like all the other nations instead of a special people of God

They wanted to be like the heathen nations around them! Reluctantly, Samuel took their request for a king before God. The remaining verses in 1 Samuel 8 report how God responded to such a request. Their desire for a king would be granted, however, it came with a warning. Their monarchy would come with a deep price. One more thing that was included in God's "Master Plan," David became a part of their future by this decision, as well as Christ the Ultimate King of Glory.

¹¹ And he said, This will be the manner of the king that shall reign over you: He will take your sons, and appoint *them* for himself, for his chariots, and *to be* his horsemen; and *some* shall run before his chariots. ¹² And he will appoint him captains over thousands, and captains over fifties; and *will set them* to ear his ground, and to reap his harvest, and to make his instruments of war, and instruments of his chariots. ¹³ And he will take your daughters *to be* confectionaries, and *to be* cooks, and *to be* bakers. ¹⁴ And he will take your fields, and your vineyards, and your oliveyards, *even* the best *of them*, and give *them* to his servants. ¹⁵ And he will take the tenth of your seed, and of your vineyards, and give to his officers, and to his servants. ¹⁶ And he will take your menservants, and your maidservants, and your goodliest young men, and your asses, and put *them* to his work. ¹⁷ He will take the tenth of your sheep: and ye shall be his servants. ¹⁸ And ye shall cry out in that day because of your king which ye shall have chosen you; and the LORD will not hear you in that day. ¹⁹ Nevertheless the people refused to obey the voice of Samuel; and they said, Nay; but we will have a king over us;   *1 Sam 8:11-19*

The rejection of Samuel's warning not to have a king confirmed the people's rejection not of Samuel, but of God himself.

At or near this time, the 390 years of rebelling referred to in Ezekiel 4 begins. A generally accepted date by Biblical historians for this event is 1112 – 1108 B.C. This allows us to be more certain of the event, which ended the 390 years of Israel's sin. The Assyrian conquest, covered in detail in 2 Kings 17:6, results in the captivity and later scattering of Israel throughout the world. (not Judah) The conquest takes place in 721 – 722 B.C. If God said their sin lasted 390 years, then we can be sure the rejection of God by requesting a king "like the other nations" and it took place around the years of 1112 – 1111 B.C. This also confirms the request for a king is the event, which began the years of sin.

At this point, it is well to understand the accuracy of God. What is a year, and what is a time? We need to understand this when considering specific times, which God uses. A 30 day month and a 12 month year is most often accepted and confirmed in several places in scripture. Genesis 7 & 8 gives us a good reference point for the comparison of days and months.

> [11] In the six hundredth year of Noah's life, in the second month, the seventeenth day of the month, the same day were all the fountains of the great deep broken up, and the windows of heaven were opened. *Gen 7:11*

> [24] And the waters prevailed upon the earth an hundred and fifty days. *Gen 7:24*

> [3] And the waters returned from off the earth continually: and after the end of the hundred and fifty days the waters were abate. [4] And the ark rested in the seventh month, on the seventeenth day of the month, upon the mountains of Ararat. *Gen 8:3-4*

Simply counting from the 17th day of the 2nd month, adding 150 days, which ended on the 7th day of the 7th month, we find that the flood lasted five months exactly. Each month consisted of a length of 30 days.

This example from scripture establishes a thirty-day month and a twelve-month year in the Hebrew Calendar.[13] Scripture also establishes what a "time" is. Both Daniel and Revelation use the word "time, times and half-time." In these prophecies, a time is a year of 360 days, not 365 days. In understanding prophetic scriptures, it is imperative to understand the difference in a 360-day year and a 365-day year.

---

[13] The calendar we now use, and often impose upon scripture, is the "Gregorian Calendar" developed by Pope Gregory XIII in 1582 to allow for a "leap year."

A confirming example can be found in Revelation 13: 3-5, a prophecy of an event that is now history and lasted exactly 1260 lunar years. The prophecy uses the term "forty and two months" in reference to the beast.

> [3] And I saw one of his heads as it were wounded to death; and his deadly wound was healed: and all the world wondered after the beast. [4] And they worshipped the dragon which gave power unto the beast: and they worshipped the beast, saying, Who *is* like unto the beast? who is able to make war with him? [5] And there was given unto him a mouth speaking great things and blasphemies; and power was given unto him to continue forty *and* two months. *Rev 13:2-5*

Equating the beast of Revelation 13 with the Roman Empire, the method of time interpretation can be tested.

1. Rome fell in stages from the early AD 400's to the mid AD 500's.

   a. The Vandals from 429 to 493 which ruled most of the empire

   b. The Huruli also ruled a part of the empire from 476 to 493

   c. The Ostrogoths from 493 – 554 ruled of the empire

In AD 554, Justinian restored the Imperial Roman Empire and recognized the supremacy of the Roman Pope. The beast (Rome) that received the deadly wound from the nations or tribes as outlined above, and the beast was not ruling at the time due to the deadly wound that was later healed under Justinian in AD 554. *And I saw one of his heads as it were wounded to death; and his deadly wound was healed: and all the world wondered after the beast.* Rev 13:3 . Rome again ruled! This wound lasted from AD 476 until AD 554. Revelation 13:5 continues the description and duration of the Beast's power. *And there was given unto him a mouth speaking great things and blasphemies; and power was given unto him to continue forty and two months* Rev 13:5 Keep in mind the timing of this event is after the deadly wound is healed. This forty-two months ended in 1814 (never to be restored) when Napoleon's army was defeated at Waterloo. "So closed a government that dated from Augustus Caesar." (West; Holy Roman Empire, Page 377) The events spoken of in Revelation 12:6 as a-thousand two-hundred and three-score days (1260 days) is referred to in further detail as lasting a "time times and a half a time." The same event lasts continually for 1260 years.

Daniel 12:7 further confirms that "time times and a half time refers to years.

> And I heard the man clothed in linen, which was upon the waters of the river, when he held up his right hand and his left hand unto heaven, and sware by him that liveth for ever that it shall be for a time, times, and an half; and when he shall have accomplished to scatter the power of the holy people, all these things shall be finished. Dan 12:7

RIGHTLY DIVIDING
THE WORD - 101

There is so much misunderstanding of basic scripture truth regarding the Kingdom of Israel and the Kingdom of Judah. Especially in the identification of what qualifies a person to be considered a "Jew" or "Jewish." It is not as simple as it may seem, and therefore a detailed explanation is in order.

It is interesting to note that the terms "Israel," "People of Israel," Children of Israel," and the like are mentioned at least 259[14] times in the Bible from Genesis 34 to II Kings 16:6. It is in this passage of II Kings 16:6 where the term "Jew" is first used in scripture. Unfortunately, the term "Jew" is commonly, and all to consistently, misused today to describe the Hebrew people prior to the events of II Kings 16:6. It is bad enough for secular sources such as "The History Channel" to misuse the term, however, prominent Christian Writers and Pastors are guilty of the same mistake.

Hal Lindsey and Tim LaHaye are examples of Christian writers who constantly use variations of the word "Jew" in the wrong context. Millions of books have doubtlessly been sold replete with the use of "Jew" in a general term to be synonymous with all Israel.

John Hagee, a world-renowned pastor and writer whose work I greatly admire, misused the term "Jew" in his writing. In his book, <u>Final Dawn Over Jerusalem</u>, on page 34 he writes, "as the Hebrews crossed the Red Sea, God drowned the sons of the Egyptians en mass as they

---

[14] King James Version used for count

pursued the <u>Jews</u>."   Brother Hagee's love for the Jewish People and the Land of Israel is obvious in his work. Therefore, I am embarrassed to call him out on this, but I want to show that even men I admire and whose work I appreciate, have made this mistake. In this particular instance, Hagee is apparently referring to the text found in Exodus 14.

> [22] And the children of Israel went into the midst of the sea upon the dry *ground*: and the waters *were* a wall unto them on their right hand, and on their left. [23] And the Egyptians pursued, and went in after them to the midst of the sea, *even* all Pharaoh's horses, his chariots, and his horsemen. Ex 14:22-23

A summary of the event is found a few verses later.

> [30] Thus the LORD saved Israel that day out of the hand of the Egyptians; and Israel saw the Egyptians dead upon the sea shore. [31] And Israel saw that great work which the LORD did upon the Egyptians: and the people feared the LORD, and believed the LORD, and his servant Moses.
>
> Ex 14:30-31

As you can see, neither passage includes any mention of "Hebrew" or "Jews." Only "Israel" or "Children of Israel" are mentioned. This group includes of all Israel, each of the Tribes including Judah. Then in Chapter 15 we read:

> [1] Then sang Moses and the children of Israel this song unto the LORD, and spake, saying, I will sing unto the LORD, for he hath triumphed gloriously: the horse and his rider hath he thrown into the sea. Ex 15:1

The Jews must not have learned the song yet!

Why? The term "Jew" mainly came about as a term referring only to the Tribe of Judah. (Judah was the fourth son of Jacob and Leah) Later, the term came to include the Tribe of Benjamin and part of Levi. Judah never included the other Ten Tribes, the Nation of Israel, or the House of Israel. Prior to the events of 1 Kings 11 & 12, chapters often referred to in this book in discussion of the division of the Tribes into a Northern and Southern Kingdom, Judah was just a part of the whole House of Israel.

It is important to take note here that the Tribe of Judah was designated as the Scepter Line of Blessing. The Scepter Line runs through Christ. See Genesis 49:10 and Matthew 1:1-18 for confirmation of this.

Judah then, was a part of the Children of Israel (Jacob) when discussing their time in Egypt and through the Exile. However, to lump all the Tribes together during this period and call them "Jews" is completely inaccurate. Furthermore, this inaccuracy leads to a whole host of misunderstanding and erroneous interpretation of God's Word.

It is a concern over insuring an accurate interpretation of Prophecy and an understanding of the Kingdom of God, which led me to use Hagee's book as an example of the danger of using the wrong term. For instance, if the term "Jew" is not accurate until after 2 Kings 16, how accurate is it for Christians to praise Abraham, Isaac, Jacob, David, Jesus, Paul and so on as "Dead Jews of the past?" (Final Dawn over Jerusalem page 17)

- Abraham was a native of the Ur of the Chaldeans – Gen. 11:32
  o His background was pagan – Josh. 24:2-3
- Isaac was born in Gerar (Genesis 20) and lived approximately 1000 years before there was ever a Jew
- Jacob was the beginning of what was now known

as the "Children of Israel," following God's changing of Jacob's name to Israel

- David was of the Tribe of Judah (Scepter Line) but lived too early to be called a Jew
- Jesus <u>was</u> a Jew! Finally the writer gets it correct
- Paul was a Jew of the Tribe of Benjamin

Simply put, getting it right two times out of six is not good enough for an author and teacher of the caliber of Bro. Hagee.

One last example, "The Jewish people have been persecuted throughout history. They were enslaved in Egypt," (wrong) "deported by the Assyrians," (wrong) "attacked by Nebuchadnezzar," (right on this one). (Hagee, page 43) One out of three on such an important point is still not good enough.

Let me conclude this by showing who the Assyrians did deport, and I believe it will show why accuracy in using the term "Jew" is important.

> [13] Yet the LORD testified against Israel, and against Judah, by all the prophets, *and by* all the seers, saying, Turn ye from your evil ways, and keep my commandments *and* my statutes, according to all the law which I commanded your fathers, and which I sent to you by my servants the prophets. [14] Notwithstanding they would not hear, but hardened their necks, like to the neck of their fathers, that did not believe in the LORD their God.
>
> [15] And they rejected his statutes, and his covenant that he made with their fathers, and his testimonies which he testified against them; and they followed vanity, and became vain, and went after the heathen that *were* round about them, *concerning* whom the LORD had charged them, that they should not do like them.
>
> [16] And they left all the commandments of the LORD their God, and made them molten images, *even* two calves, and made a grove, and worshipped all the host of heaven, and served Baal. [17] And they caused their sons and their

daughters to pass through the fire, and used divination and enchantments, and sold themselves to do evil in the sight of the LORD, to provoke him to anger. [18] Therefore the LORD was very angry with Israel, and removed them out of his sight: <u>there was none left but the Tribe of Judah only</u>. [19] Also Judah kept not the commandments of the LORD their God, but walked in the statutes of Israel which they made. [20] And the LORD rejected all the seed of Israel, and afflicted them, and delivered them into the hand of spoilers, until he had cast them out of his sight. [21] For he rent Israel from the house of David; and they made Jeroboam the son of Nebat king: and Jeroboam drave Israel from following the LORD, and made them sin a great sin. [22] For the children of Israel walked in all the sins of Jeroboam which he did; they departed not from them; [23] Until the LORD removed Israel out of his sight, as he had said by all his servants the prophets. So was Israel carried away out of their own land to Assyria unto this day. 2 Kings 17:13-23

Consider the following concerning this passage.

- God condemned both Israel and Judah – 13-15
- The condemning is aimed more toward Israel than Judah because of the order of events – 16
- God removed Israel to Assyria and left Judah (the Jews) – 18

Later, Judah (including parts of Benjamin and Levi) was enslaved by Nebuchadnezzar. This event is recorded in Jeremiah 37 and 2 Kings 24. Let me emphasize that Judah was not taken captive into Assyria along with Israel in 2 Kings 17.

Please be aware that this writer intends no disrespect toward other writers previously mentioned. Rather, it is the intent to respectfully point out the danger of such errors as they apply to the understanding of God's Word. This is meant to enhance a better understanding of prophecy with historical accuracy. The Biblical fact is, God deals with Judah and Israel separately, not as a collective "the Jews." Incorrectly lumping them together fosters many erroneous beliefs and doctrines, especially concerning End Time prophecy. Beloved brothers and sisters in Christ take note: God's Word can be understood by a Child of God by rightly dividing and confirming that understanding in the "mouth of two or more witnesses" within God's Word.

One final note concerning scripture references to Israel and Jews: At the time of 2 Kings 16:6 when the term "Jew" first appears, Israel and Judah are fighting.

THE LOST
TEN TRIBES

Not Really!

Lost! What a terrible meaning we in modern Christendom attach to the word "lost". We further attach the term "The Ten Lost Tribes" to Israel after they were conquered by Assyria in B.C. 721. To whom are they lost? Certainly, they are not lost to God. God had decreed that he would cast them out of his sight in 2 Kings 12:23. Nowhere else, however, does God say they are "lost," *but* "hidden," or that he had "turned his back on them." They may have been out of his sight, but never were they out of his mind. Several prophetic scriptures confirm that God always intended to keep his promises to the Sons of Jacob. Isaiah, Jeremiah, Ezekiel, Hosea, Zachariah, and Amos are among the prophets writing of a future restoration for Israel, separate from Judah. Daniel points out that the, "wise shall understand." Space limits prohibit a complete listing of all the scriptures relevant to this topic, but a few are required for clarity and understanding.

Isaiah

In Isaiah 11 begins with a prediction of the first coming of Christ and continues in a condensed form to prophecy events through to the Last Days. This covers a period of over 2000 years. Read the entire chapter as a whole, with particular attention to verses 9-13.

> [1] And there shall come forth a rod out of the stem of Jesse, and a Branch shall grow out of his roots: [2] And the spirit of the LORD shall rest upon him, the spirit of wisdom and understanding, the spirit of counsel and might, the spirit of knowledge and of the fear of the LORD; [3] And shall make him of quick understanding in the fear of the LORD: and

he shall not judge after the sight of his eyes, neither reprove after the hearing of his ears: ⁴ But with righteousness shall he judge the poor, and reprove with equity for the meek of the earth: and he shall smite the earth with the rod of his mouth, and with the breath of his lips shall he slay the wicked.⁵ And righteousness shall be the girdle of his loins, and faithfulness the girdle of his reins. ⁶ The wolf also shall dwell with the lamb, and the leopard shall lie down with the kid; and the calf and the young lion and the fatling together; and a little child shall lead them.

⁷ And the cow and the bear shall feed; their young ones shall lie down together: and the lion shall eat straw like the ox. ⁸ And the sucking child shall play on the hole of the asp, and the weaned child shall put his hand on the cockatrice' den. ⁹ <u>They shall not hurt nor destroy in all my holy mountain: for the earth shall be full of the knowledge of the LORD.</u> as the waters cover the sea.

¹⁰ And in that day there shall be a root of Jesse. which shall stand for an ensign of the people: to it shall the Gentiles seek: and his rest shall be glorious. ¹¹ And it shall come to pass in that day, that the Lord shall set his hand again the second time to recover the remnant of his people, which shall be left, from Assyria, and from Egypt, and from Pathros. and from Gush, and from Elam. and from Shinar. and from Hamath. and from the islands of the sea. ¹² And he shall set up an ensign for the nations, and shall assemble the outcasts of Israel, and gather together the dispersed of Judah from the four corners of the earth. ¹³ The envy also of Ephraim shall depart, and the adversaries of Judah shall be cut off: Ephraim shall not envy Judah, and Judah shall not vex Ephraim. ¹⁴ But they shall fly upon the shoulders of the Philistines toward the west; they shall spoil them of the east together: they shall lay their hand upon Edom and Moab; and the children of Ammon shall obey them. ¹⁵ And the LORD shall utterly destroy the tongue of the Egyptian sea; and with his mighty wind shall he shake his hand over the river, and shall smite it in the seven streams, and make men go over dryshod. ¹⁶ And there shall be an highway for the remnant of his people, which shall be left, from Assyria; like as it was to Israel in the day that he came up out of the land of Egypt. Isaiah 11:1-13

A major theme of this passage is the re-gathering of Israel and Judah together. Not only will they be together, but also the nature of their existence together will be that of peace. No longer adversaries who envy one another, the two shall be in harmony as brothers.

Jeremiah

> The LORD said also unto me in the days of Josiah the king, Hast thou seen that which backsliding Israel hath done? She is gone up upon every high mountain and under every green tree, and there hath played the harlot. [7] And I said after she had done all these things, Turn thou unto me. But she returned not. And her treacherous sister Judah saw it. [8] And I saw, when for all the causes whereby backsliding Israel committed adultery I had put her away, and given her a bill of divorce; yet her treacherous sister Judah feared not, but went and played the harlot also. [9] And it came to pass through the lightness of her whoredom, that she defiled the land, and committed adultery with stones and with stocks.[10] And yet for all this her treacherous sister Judah hath not turned unto me with her whole heart, but feignedly, saith the LORD. [11] And the LORD said unto me, The backsliding Israel hath justified herself more than treacherous Judah. Jer 3:6-11

In Jeremiah, the Lord unveils a vision in Chapter 3 of Israel and Judah after both sinned and turned from Him. Israel completely turned from God approximately 130 years before Judah, already being in Assyrian captivity by the time of Judah's defeat and captivity, (see 2 Kings 17) Judah was in Babylonian Captivity, which is where Jeremiah found himself at the time of God's vision. Through Jeremiah, God condemned Israel while being somewhat lenient, even giving a backhanded compliment to Judah. However, Judah did not heed the warning of God, missing out on the chance God was giving because there was at least a measure of seeking the Lord remaining in Judah. Judah's failure to return to God whole-heartedly resulted in Judah sharing the punishment of Israel. Both provoked the Lord until both were punished. An important point here is that they were punished for their sin, not destroyed. Such punishment came because of sin, not because God desired evil for either Israel or Judah. For Judah, the punishment lasted seventy years. For Israel, punishment continued for a much longer period (more of this later).

Furthermore, the prophet portrayed a future time of re-gathering of the two nations into a nation defined by peace and harmony in the Last Days. Read all of Jeremiah 3 for a complete understanding of the prophet's message. Note especially his words in verses 17 & 18 as he speaks specifically of the Last Days.

> [17] At that time they shall call Jerusalem the throne of the LORD; and all the nations shall be gathered unto it, to the name of the LORD, to Jerusalem: neither shall they walk any more after the imagination of their evil heart. [18] In those days the house of Judah shall walk with the house of Israel, and they shall come together out of the land of the north to the land that I have given for an inheritance unto your fathers. Jer3:17-18

Again, God speaks through Jeremiah of a time when both nations shall come back together. The point of reunification brings them to the land God, "gave unto your fathers." This speaks of both a time of reunification and a physical re-gathering of both nations into the land of Canaan. Canaan stands as the only land promised to all the children of Israel jointly. A point, which modern Christianity often fails to recognize, is that the land which would produce the Birthright Blessing was never promised to Judah. This failure is a result of not recognizing the clear distinction between the House of Judah and the Kingdom of Israel in prophecy. A point made clear by the prophet Ezekiel.

> [15] The word of the LORD came again unto me, saying, [16] Moreover, thou son of man, take thee one stick, and write upon it, For Judah, and for the children of Israel his companions: then take another stick, and write upon it, For Joseph, the stick of Ephraim, and for all the house of

Israel his companions: [17] And join them one to another into one stick; and they shall become one in thine hand. [18] And when the children of thy people shall speak unto thee, saying, Wilt thou not shew us what thou meanest by these?

[19] Say unto them, Thus saith the Lord GOD; Behold, I will take the stick of Joseph, which is in the hand of Ephraim, and the tribes of Israel his fellows, and will put them with him, even with the stick of Judah, and make them one stick, and they shall be one in mine hand. [20] And the sticks whereon thou writest shall be in thine hand before their eyes. [21] And say unto them, Thus saith the Lord GOD; Behold, I will take the children of Israel from among the heathen, whither they be gone, and will gather them on every side, and bring them into their own land. [22] And I will make them one nation in the land upon the mountains of Israel; and one king shall be king to them all: and they shall be no more two nations, neither shall they be divided into two kingdoms any more at all: [23] Neither shall they defile themselves any more with their idols, nor with their detestable things, nor with any of their transgressions: but I will save them out of all their dwellingplaces, wherein they have sinned, and will cleanse them: so shall they be my people, and I will be their God. [24] And David my servant shall be king over them; and they all shall have one shepherd: they shall also walk in my judgments, and observe my statutes, and do them. [25] And they shall dwell in the land that I have given unto Jacob my servant, wherein your fathers have dwelt; and they shall dwell therein, even they, and their children, and their children's children for ever: and my servant David shall be their prince for ever. [26] Moreover I will make a covenant of peace with them; it shall be an everlasting covenant with them: and I will place them, and multiply them, and will set my sanctuary in the midst of them for evermore. [27] My tabernacle also shall be with them: yea, I will be their God, and they shall be my people. [28] And the heathen shall know that I the LORD do sanctify Israel, when my sanctuary shall be in the midst of them for evermore. Ezek 37:15-28

Hosea

The book of Hosea is almost entirely about Israel. Only a very few references can be found regarding Judah. When they are found, it is obvious that they are two distinct nations. Hosea wrote in approximately 765 BC, years prior to the time when each nation separately fell into Assyrian and Babylon captivity. However within his message, primarily to Israel the Birthright Nation, the many references regarding Ephraim confirm this truth. Hosea even tells the direction Ephraim moved in following their Assyrian Captivity. [1] *Ephraim feedeth on wind, and followeth after the east wind: he daily increaseth lies and desolation; and they do make a covenant with the Assyrians, and oil is carried into Egypt.* (Hosea 12:1) *The East Wind blows from the east toward the west.* Chapter 7 verse 8 states, *Ephraim, he hath mixed himself among the people; Ephraim is a cake not turned.* In other words, he is not yet complete.

In Genesis 49:22, previously referenced, Joseph is a fruitful bough by walls whose branches run over the walls. What does this mean? Recall that the Birthright was conferred upon Ephraim and Manasseh jointly through Joseph. History shows that they stayed together for a long time and then that one would be a "company of nations" (Ephraim). The other, (Manasseh), would of itself become a "great nation." This is an example of why Genesis 49 is such an important key to understanding the plight of the children of Jacob. Verse 22 of Genesis 49 seemingly becomes a prophetic utterance by Jacob of a time when from the "company of nations" one branches off to become a "great nation" by itself.

Returning to the original thought of the reunification of the two separate nations of Israel and Judah in the Last Days, only two additional verses in Hosea need referencing to confirm the truth.

¹⁰ Yet the number of the children of Israel shall be as the sand of the sea, which cannot be measured nor numbered; and it shall come to pass, that in the place where it was said unto them, Ye are not my people, there it shall be said unto them, Ye are the sons of the living God.

¹¹ Then shall the children of Judah and the children of Israel be gathered together, and appoint themselves one head, and they shall come up out of the land: for great shall be the day of Jezreel. Hosea 1:10-11

Two nations are definitively shown here coming together under one head, Christ. Allow me to suggest that you study the entire book of Hosea, taking note of all the scriptures referring directly to Ephraim. As you do so, remember that it is Ephraim to whom God promised to make a "company of nations."

Amos

In Amos 1:1, the author starts by identifying himself and the time of his writing. In verse 2, he immediately jumps to a prophecy of the Last Days. ² *And he said, The LORD will roar from Zion, and utter his voice from Jerusalem; and the habitations of the shepherds shall mourn, and the top of Carmel shall wither.* (Amos 1:2) Joel 3:16 uses the exact phrase, "shall roar out of Zion," clearly speaking of the Last Days. Zechariah 14:4, speaking of the same event as Joel's refers to "the top of Mt. Carmel shall wither" when he says,

⁴ And his feet shall stand in that day upon the mount of Olives, which is before Jerusalem on the east, and the mount of Olives shall cleave in the midst thereof toward the east and toward the west, and there shall be a very great valley; and half of the mountain shall remove toward the north, and half of it toward the south. Zech 14:4

Regarding the Birthright Nation during this time, Amos addresses the House of Israel in Chapter 5. ¹ *Hear ye this word which I take up against you, even a lamentation, O house of*

Israel. (Amos 5:1). From here, he traces the path of The House of Israel. Consider these selected passages.

- Concerning God's mercy toward the Remnant: *[15] Hate the evil, and love the good, and establish judgment in the gate: it may be that the LORD God of hosts will be gracious unto the remnant of Joseph* Amos 5:15
- Concerning the afflictions of Joseph: *[7] Therefore now shall they go captive with the first that go captive, and the banquet of them that stretched themselves shall be removed* Amos 6:7
- Chapter 9 provides one of Amos' clearest views of Joseph as the recipient of the Birthright Blessing and God's watchful eye over them.

Behold, the eyes of the Lord GOD are upon the sinful kingdom, and I will destroy it from off the face of the earth; saving that I will not utterly destroy the house of Jacob, saith the LORD.9 For, lo, I will command, and I will sift the house of Israel among all nations, like as corn is sifted in a sieve, yet shall not the least grain fall upon the earth. 10 All the sinners of my people shall die by the sword, which say, The evil shall not overtake nor prevent us. In that day will I raise up the tabernacle of David that is fallen, and close up the breaches thereof; and I will raise up his ruins, and I will build it as in the days of old:12 That they may possess the land.

The remnant of Edom, and of all the heathen, which are called by my name, saith the LORD that doeth this. 13 Behold, the days come, saith the LORD, that the plowman shall overtake the reaper, and the treader of grapes him that soweth seed; and the mountains shall drop sweet wine, and all the hills shall melt. 14 And I will bring again the captivity of my people of Israel, and they shall build the waste cities, and inhabit them; and they shall plant vineyards, and drink the wine thereof; they shall also make gardens, and eat the fruit of them. And I will plant them upon their land, and they shall no more be pulled up out of their land which I have given them, saith the LORD thy God. Amos 9:8-15

God will scatter and re-gather the remnant of Jacob. As identified in 5:15, He is speaking of Joseph after being sifted throughout the earth under His watchful eye. This is further confirmed by Jesus when he said in Matthew 13:44, that God had found his treasure (see Exodus 19:5-7, Psalms 135:4) which had been hidden in the field (world). Upon finding the treasure, he gave all he had, his son, in order to purchase the field. In these three scriptures, we find the only thing ever referred to as God's treasure, and that is Israel.

Zechariah

> ⁶ And I will strengthen the house of Judah, and I will save the house of Joseph, and I will bring them again to place them; for I have mercy upon them: and they shall be as though I had not cast them off: for I am the LORD their God, and will hear them. ⁷ And they of Ephraim shall be like a mighty man, and their heart shall rejoice as through wine: yea, their children shall see it, and be glad; their heart shall rejoice in the LORD. ⁸ I will hiss for them, and gather them; for I have redeemed them: and they shall increase as they have increased. ⁹ And I will sow them among the people: and they shall remember me in far countries; and they shall live with their children, and turn again.
>
> ¹⁰ I will bring them again also out of the land of Egypt, and gather them out of Assyria; and I will bring them into the land of Gilead and Lebanon; and place shall not be found for them. ¹¹ And he shall pass through the sea with affliction, and shall smite the waves in the sea, and all the deeps of the river shall dry up: and the pride of Assyria shall be brought down, and the sceptre of Egypt shall depart away. ¹² And I will strengthen them in the LORD; and they shall walk up and down in his name, saith the LORD. Zech 10:6-12

The proceeding verses, taken from one of the most prophetic books of the Old Testament, serves to point out that God will gather and reunite Judah and Israel. They will be called together in the Last Days, living in peace and harmony in the land of Canaan. This idea is very discomforting to many who claim they are a "New Testament Church," believing the Old Testament is for the Jews only, while the New Testament is for the church of today. Others who do not share the New Testament Church beliefs in their entirety, must be asking themselves, "what about the church? How could it possibly fit into this truth? I am glad you asked. The chapter, "What About the Church," covers this in detail.

BIRTHRIGHT NATIONS: THE BEGINNING

During the late 1700's and early 1800's, the United States separated from British rule and was on its way to becoming the most powerful and wealthiest nation on earth. Such wealth and power like that promised to Manasseh in Genesis 48:19, greater than that of his older brother. Manasseh (United States) had separated from his brother Ephraim (United Kingdom) in 1792.

The United States purchased, what was later to become the most valuable piece of real estate per square foot in the world, from the Indians for a few beads. The Louisiana Purchase in 1803 doubled the size of the U.S. and the westward movement began. Gold was discovered in California, the rich farmlands of the Midwest were beginning to produce in abundance. The coal fields in the Eastern U.S. was yielding their bountiful wealth, permitting an industrial expansion of the North Eastern states the likes the world had never seen before.

Soon Great Britain's Empire was such that "the sun never set on her holdings." Between the United States and Great Britain, they owned almost three fourths of the world's wealth and resources in a very short time. All of the promises God had made to Israel (Not Judah) could be seen being rapidly poured upon these two nations.

- A nation and a company of nations – Gen. 49:19
- Shall possess the gates of his enemies – Gen. 22:17
- Multiply thy seed as the stars of heaven and sands of seashore
- Thy seed shall be as the dust of the earth – spread to the <u>west</u> – east – north – south -Gen. 28:14

- In thy seed shall all of the nations be blessed – Gen. 28:14
- A nation and a company of nations shall be of the promise and kings shall come out of thy loins Gen 35:11

> In 1846 American rebels raised the "Bear" flag of California, conquered the Mexican Army, and took that territory, thereby expanding the United States from the Atlantic to the Pacific Ocean. The state of Florida was acquired from Spain and the statehood continued westward. More? The transcontinental railroad was joined at Pomatory Point, Utah in 1867 and the west was opened up to eastern commerce.

> Robert Fulton operated the first steamboat in 1803, exactly 2520 years from the time God cast the birthright nation "out of his sight" (2 Kings 17). During those very years of the early 19th century Britain and America came into the "gates of their enemies" and those who hate them" (Gen. 24:60). Gibraltar, the Suez Canal, the Gulf of Singapore, became a vital part of their possessions, and most remain today. In Deut. 33:17 we read, *His glory is like the firstling* (firstborn – birthright holder) *of his bullock and his horns are like the horns of the unicorn.* Is it a coincidence that the national seal of Great Britain is a unicorn?

- And he set Ephraim before Manasseh and his seed shall become a multitude of nations – Gen. 48:19
- Blessed in the city, in the field, blessed be the fruit of thy body, fruit on the ground, of cattle of flocks of sheep – Deut. 28:3-5

This is a condensed list of the promises offered to the house of Israel and specified to Joseph and his two sons.

If there is more clarity needed, in Deut. 33 (previously quoted), Moses gives his farewell address to Israel. It is worthwhile to re-read the entire chapter. Here we will repeat it in its entirety the blessings he passed on to Joseph under the authority of God.

> [13] And of Joseph he said, Blessed of the LORD *be* his land, for the precious things of heaven, for the dew, and for the deep that coucheth beneath, [14] And for the precious fruits *brought forth* by the sun, and for the precious things put forth by the moon, [15] And for the chief things of the ancient mountains, and for the precious things of the lasting hills, [16] And for the precious things of the earth and fulness thereof, and *for* the good will of him that dwelt in the bush: let *the blessing* come upon the head of Joseph, and upon the top of the head of him *that was* separated from his brethren. [17] His glory *is like* the firstling of his bullock, and his horns *are like* the horns of unicorns: with them he shall push the people together to the ends of the earth: and they *are* the ten thousands of Ephraim, and they *are* the thousands of Manasseh. Deut 33:13-17

There were other events taking place in these two fledgling nations that met the qualifications for God to once more pour out his material blessings after withholding these promises for over 2500 years. People were turning to God and true worship. Remember as far back as 1620 the pilgrims sailed to the New World to escape the religious intolerance of England who at the time was under the heel of the pope. Sufficient to say at this time is, that the defeat of Napoleon in 1814 gave additional freedom for the advance of Protestantism, which was already moving the Methodist all over Europe. A movement that had its origin in a little group of students at Oxford University (led by John Wesley, Charles Wesley and George Whitfield. These three men led the most remarkable itinerant ministry in the history of Protestantism). Their message to the common man was much like the Puritans of earlier years.

Calvin spread the gospel in France, the Rhine valley, the Netherlands, England and Scotland, and eventually reached America. The Huguenots of France was slowly re-establishing the truths of the Bible that had been suppressed in France for Centuries.

However most of the British Isles (Ephraim the company of nations) was still a religious monarchy (Church of England) though no longer under the pope, it still lacked true religious freedom. That was what the pilgrimage in 1620 was all about.

The fledgling thirteen colonies wanted true freedom and religious freedom especially. In the very years predicted 1445 to 1783 the colonies of the new world sprang "over the wall," they separated and a "great nations" was born (Manasseh) (Gen. 48.19). With its parentage in the "Company of Nations," (Ephraim) the religious freedom so fervently sought by these pioneers began with men like Roger Williams and was expanded by great missionaries like David Brainerd, a Yale educated Congregationalist minister. He spent most of his adult life carrying the cause of Christ to the Delaware Indians.

All of New England, including Yale College, was being swept by a vast revival that historians refer to as the first Great Awakening. On October 2, 1792, William Carey, along with other evangelistic minded Baptists formed the first Baptist Missionary Society to send the Gospel to other nations. Carey's influence in England was responsible for the printing of Bibles to be sent to India.

"On a clear morning I have seen in Africa the rising smoke from a thousand villages where Jesus Christ is utterly unknown." So said Robert Moffat, pioneer missionary and Biblical translator in South Africa. This statement struck the very heart of David Livingston and proved to be the turning point in his life. The London Missionary Society accepted the appointment of Livingston in November 1840 and he sailed to the "dark continent." He made many trips into the interior of the continent for missionary work and exploration. His exploits were so profound and newsworthy that in 1871 after over thirty years work in the Dark Continent, the New York Herald sent Henry M. Stanley to find Livingston. He finally located him in a tiny village in Tanganyika. Livingston was tall, frail and near death. Upon approaching Livingstone, Henry Stanley uttered that now famous statement, "Dr. Livingstone I presume."

On May 1, 1873, Dr. Livingstone died after a lifetime of service in his beloved country near Lake Bangweols and his heart was buried there by the natives. His body was preserved and was eventually buried in Westminster Abby with full national honors. However, his greatest honor was that he was ranked as one of the "men who made missions."

The first missionary to be sent from American was born Adoniram Judson August 9, 1788 in Massachusetts. An extremely intelligent child, he was reading fluently in Hebrew and Greek before the age of ten. His parents insisted he get a 'proper" education. Thinking that both Howard and Yale Universities were both too "liberal' they chose Brown University in Rhode Island. His education at Brown did not turn out as his Puritan father had hoped. Adoniram quickly became agnostic much to the disbelief of all who knew him. He traveled the theatrical circuit for a time but that too left him totally disillusioned. A chance incident of watching a sick man die in an inn where he had lodged for the night changed his life. His death cries caused great reflections in his life and upbringing as he thought, "What if that were I?" Shortly after he returned home no longer an agnostic but with a faith that endured until his death. Adoniram enrolled in a new seminary at Andover where he came across a printed sermon by Claudius Buchanan, a chaplain in India, entitled "The Star in the East." This was the inspiration for his famous missionary journey to India, which began in February 1812, thus opening the Gospel of Christ to India. He suffered untold hardships, imprisonment, and illness that finally took his life, but he left a legacy of an open door to India.

Such was the legacy of some of the thousands of men and women who gave their all to tell the world about Christ. All this springing from the two birthright nations, which put God first, a pre-requisite for him to fulfill his unconditional promise after withholding it for over 2500 years because of Israel's sin.

As further proof of God's hand in the blessings of these two nations coming into power at the beginning of the 19th century is that no other nation on earth had founded their nation on their knees seeking God and freedom of worship as Britain and America did.

Men like Washington, the signers of the Declaration of Independence and the Constitution, Lincoln and scores of others proclaimed that God was the true founder of this nation. Perhaps they knew the real source of their blessings that is so plainly taught in God's Word. In a Proclamation by Abraham Lincoln calling for a national day of prayer and humiliation on April 30, 1863, he stated;

> ... It is the duty of nations as well as of men, to own their dependence upon the overruling power of God, to confess their sins and transgressions, in humble sorrow, yet with assured hope that genuine repentance will lead to mercy and pardon: and to recognize the sublime truth, announced

in Holy Scriptures and proven by all history, that those nations only are blessed whose God is the Lord.

... We have been the recipients of the choicest bounties of Heaven. We have been preserved, these many years, in peace and prosperity. We have grown in numbers, wealth and power, as no other nation has ever grown. But we have forgotten God. We have forgotten the gracious hand which preserved us in peace, and multiplied and enriched and strengthened us; and we have vainly imagined, in the deceitfulness of our hearts, that all these blessings were produced by some superior wisdom and virtue of our own.[15]

Blessed is the nation whose God is the Lord and the people he has chosen for his own inheritance. (Ps. 33:12) What a powerful, confirming proclamation. In the original Hebrew the words "and" and "Whom" is not in the text, and it read: *blessed is the nation when God is the Lord, the people he has chosen for his own inheritance.* This would seem to give more insight to the fact that the people who chose God as their Lord as the inheritors of his blessings. These two nations in turn have blessed the entire world through their missionary efforts as well as the sharing the material blessing they received. **It is noteworthy to see here that the blessings of the Birthright Nations made the carrying out of the Great Commission[16] possible. No other nations retained the Knowledge of God nor have the resources and desire to do so.**

---

[15] This resolution was introduced into the Senate on March 2,1863 by Senator James Harlan of Iowa, adopted by the Senate on March 3, and signed by Lincoln on March 30, 1863

[16] Matthew 28:19-20

We see a literal explosion of growth of these two nations at around the years 1800-1805. Is there anything in God's Word that might indicate this date would be the ending of God's withholding of the birthright blessing? Go back to Leviticus 26. Remembering the "day for a year' and "year for a day principle" for punishment and the withholding of blessings. Verses 14 – 17 reflect the 390-year period they rejected God and ask for a king (1111 – 721 BC) and was demonstrated by Ezekiel in chapter 4. Now God is outlining another period from the Assyrian captivity forward. Up to that time, God had continually sent his prophets to warn Israel of their sings. The prophets were ignored and often killed. This is where God said he "would cast them out of his sight." In Lev. 26:8 God gives an additional warning to Israel that covers the next period of unbelief, and in verse 21 he speaks of the intensity of their punishment.

> And if ye will not yet for all this hearken unto me, then I will punish you seven times more for your sins. *(duration*)* ¹⁹ And I will break the pride of your power; and I will make your heaven as iron, and your earth as brass: ²⁰ And your strength shall be spent in vain: for your land shall not yield her increase, neither shall the trees of the land yield their fruits. ²¹ And if ye walk contrary unto me, and will not hearken unto me; I will bring seven times more plagues upon you according to your sins. *(Intensity*) Lev 26:18-21*
> **Added for clarification*

In verse 18 God says, if you still do not listen and obey, I will punish you seven "times" more for your sins. We have already shown that "times" in prophecy often refers to years, and a year is calculated on a 360-day lunar year. Using the day for year principle, the duration for further punishment and withholding of their birthright blessings, 360 years multiplied by seven years amounts to 2520 years. The Assyrian Captivity began in the years 722 – 720 BC and the sudden emergence of Britain and the United States in "a company of nations" and a great nation began approximately 1792 to 1803. This is a historical fact as some of these major events have already been listed above. Skeptics will say this is "playing with numbers." Say on doubters and unbelievers, but this is consistent with God's Word in many places throughout scripture regarding the birthright blessing.

In verse 21 seems to refer to the intensity of their punishment during this period. Look at some of the persecutions that man inflicted upon man during that time. Space will only permit listing a few. The crusades, the inquisition, black plague and countless other tragedies were inflicted on God's people as they were scattered "sifted" throughout the nations of the world. Where did they go?

They Went That-a-way

God's Word gives us much insight into where Israel went after they spent a time in Assyrian captivity. We know they did not stay there. Amos tells us in 9:8 that they were "sifted among all nations". Hosea, who was writing to the house of Israel, (not Judah – not the Jews), said they would "abide many days without a king." Other references this "sifting" include.

- Moreover I will appoint a place for my people Israel, and will plant them, that they may dwell in a place of their own, and move no more; neither shall the children of wickedness afflict them any more, as beforetime, - 2 Sam 7:10
- Jumping ahead to the time when the throne of David (Christ) shall be established "forever" - He shall build an house for my name, and I will establish the throne of his kingdom for ever. - 2 Sam 7:13
- 1 Chronicles 17:11-14 repeats essentially the same thing.

Jeremiah was a captive in Babylon some one hundred and thirty years after Israel was taken captive. Yet he was instructed to write to the house of Israel. In chapter 3 verses 1-11 God's Word came to Jeremiah regarding the sins of both Judah and Israel. Clearly there are different messages to different nations. In Verse 12, God says, *Go and proclaim these words toward the north, and say, Return, thou backsliding Israel, saith the LORD; and I will not cause mine anger to fall upon you: for I am merciful, saith the LORD, and I will not keep anger for ever.* Jer 3:12 To clarify a truth, remember Israel had gone north but both Israel and Assyria had expanded further north and west at the time of Jeremiah's writing.

Hosea tells us in a verse already quoted, 12:1, that Ephraim (the promised company of nations) "followeth after the east wind." The east wind blows toward the west. If God's Word is true, Ephraim went west from Assyria. Now from these scriptures we find Israel (Ephraim) north and west of the land where Judah is located in the Promised Land. Hosea 11:8 God uses the name Israel and Ephraim as the same people and in verse 10. He says they shall "tremble from the west", referring to the Last Days.

We now see Israel going north and west and finally returning to Palestine from the west in the Last Days.

There is more.

THE KINGDOM OF ISRAEL

The Kingdom of Israel must be distinguished from the Thrown of David during certain periods of history. However, the Throne of David is included as a part of the Kingdom of Israel during other periods of history.

- The Kingdom of Israel includes all the 12 Tribes (sons) of Jacob from the time of the Exodus. At the beginning, the wandering tribes did not yet meet the definition of a formal Kingdom, however, they were a Kingdom in-the-making. At the time of Solomon's death the 12 Tribes engaged in a period of tribal infighting, resulting in Judah separating from the rest of the tribes. At this point in history, the 12 tribes split into two Kingdoms, Judah to forming one Kingdom, and the other 10 Tribes forming the Kingdom called Israel.
- Prior to that time, the term a most often applied to the 12 tribes was the "the whole house of Israel." This term is no longer accurate and will not be until the reuniting of Israel and Judah.
- When the term "Ephraim" is used, it refers strictly to the Birthright Line, recorded in Genesis 49, and other scriptures quoted elsewhere. Furthermore, it is used in 1 Kings 11, to identify the Tribes of Israel, or the Kingdom of Israel, given to Jeroboam of the Tribe of Ephraim. Whenever the term is substituted for "Israel", by definition excludes Judah and the Scepter Line (Throne of David), referring only to the Birthright Line.
- Amos 5:15 speaks of the remnant of Joseph that definitely excludes the Kingdom of Judah, Throne of David or the Jews. The term "Ephraim," is used many times in Hosea. When Ephraim is used in scripture, it is referring strictly to the Birthright Line and is directed at American and Great Britain in the End Times. This is confirmed by many scriptures and history.

The Throne of David

> *¹⁰ The sceptre shall not depart from Judah, nor a lawgiver from between his feet, until Shiloh come; and unto him shall the gathering of the people be.* Gen 49:10 (KJV)

A general interpretation of this passage is understood as a promise of the coming of Christ through the line of Judah. That certainly is true. The first earthly king after the rejection of God as King is recorded in 1ˢᵗ Samuel 8. This was Saul of the Tribe of Benjamin, a choice made by man and not by God. God soon rejected him and his dynasty ended before it ever got going.

> ⁴ And Abijah stood up upon mount Zemaraim, which *is* in mount Ephraim, and said, Hear me, thou Jeroboam, and all Israel; ⁵ Ought ye not to know that the LORD God of Israel gave the kingdom over Israel to David for ever, *even* to him and to his sons by a covenant of salt? 2 Chron 13:4-5 (KJV)

Samuel told Saul, that God had chosen a man after his own heart. David of the Tribe of Judah was anointed the new king of Israel. This established the royal line that would fulfill the above prophecy of Genesis 42:16.

Now, we fast forward to the time when King David is about to die. He has been a successful warrior king, but not without great sins in his life. He reigned in relative peace in Jerusalem and wanted to build a House for the Lord.

> ¹ And it came to pass, when the king sat in his house, and the LORD had given him rest round about from all his enemies; ² That the king said unto Nathan the prophet, See now, I dwell in an house of cedar, but the ark of God dwelleth within curtains. ³ And Nathan said to the king, Go, do all that *is* in thine heart; for the LORD *is* with thee.

⁴ And it came to pass that night, that the word of the LORD came unto Nathan, saying, ⁵ Go and tell my servant David, Thus saith the LORD, Shalt thou build me an house for me to dwell in? ⁶ Whereas I have not dwelt in *any* house since the time that I brought up the children of Israel out of Egypt, even to this day, but have walked in a tent and in a tabernacle

. ⁷ In all *the places* wherein I have walked with all the children of Israel spake I a word with any of the tribes of Israel, whom I commanded to feed my people Israel, saying, Why build ye not me an house of cedar?

⁸ Now therefore so shalt thou say unto my servant David, Thus saith the LORD of hosts, I took thee from the sheepcote, from following the sheep, to be ruler over my people, over Israel: ⁹ And I was with thee whithersoever thou wentest, and have cut off all thine enemies out of thy sight, and have made thee a great name, like unto the name of the great *men* that *are* in the earth. ¹⁰ Moreover I will appoint a place for my people Israel, and will plant them, that they may dwell in a place of their own, and move no more; neither shall the children of wickedness afflict them any more, as beforetime, ¹¹ And as since the time that I commanded judges *to be* over my people Israel, and have caused thee to rest from all thine enemies. Also the LORD telleth thee that he will make thee an house.

¹² And when thy days be fulfilled, and thou shalt sleep with thy fathers, I will set up thy seed after thee, which shall proceed out of thy bowels, and I will establish his kingdom. ¹³ He shall build an house for my name, and I will stablish the throne of his kingdom for ever.

¹⁴ I will be his father, and he shall be my son. If he commit iniquity, I will chasten him with the rod of men, and with the stripes of the children of men:

¹⁵ But my mercy shall not depart away from him, as I took *it* from Saul, whom I put away before thee. ¹⁶ And thine house and thy kingdom shall be established for ever before thee: thy throne shall be established for ever. 2 Sam 7:1-16

We see here a divine promise of God, which is confirmed through the ages in Genesis 49:10. The scepter and the spiritual blessings shall not depart from the Tribe of Judah until Christ comes. That within itself is an outstanding promise in light of the contemporary teachings that reflect no other understanding of its magnitude. It is important to remember here that King Saul <u>had</u> to be rejected in order for this promise to Judah to be fulfilled. Saul was of the Tribe of Benjamin. Chapter 7 of 2ⁿᵈ Samuel provides further insight into the throne of David.

- Remember, once established, it would continue until Christ came - Genesis 49:10.
- David wanted to build a house (throne), for God to do well in - 2 Samuel 7:2
- Nathan the prophet approved the plan - 7:3.
- God however said no, he would wait for David's son Solomon - 7:12.
- Solomon's throne would be established forever - 7:13
- God would be Solomon's father - symbolically replacing David - 7:14.
- If Solomon committed iniquity, he would be chastened not by God, but by men and the children of men (over a period of time). Continue to remember that David's throne is to be established forever. 7:14
- God's mercy will always be with the throne of David as established through Solomon - 7:15
- David's house, kingdom, and throne is established forever.

This amazing prophecy contains world-shaping promises, which are all for the most part, misunderstood. Contemporary Christianity often says this passage states that Christ's throne is now in heaven. I do not believe this to be a correct interpretation of scripture. Notice that the throne is established in some one who will undoubtedly sin. Certainly, this cannot be about Christ. For we must remember, he was without sin. Secondly, when this king and his future line sin, his dynasty does not end but he is chastised by men. However, it is still "established forever," and therefore still remains. If there is any part of the above quoted scriptures that the searching heart does not understand; do not worry, there is more, lots more, which I believe will help clarify it for you.

This promise was unconditional; it would not end and thus was never intended to be a just single generation. Imagine a single generation of earthly kings sitting on a throne somewhere, waiting forever until Christ comes and will then sit on the throne of David. (Not the Kingdom of Israel)

> [4] And Abijah stood up upon mount Zemaraim, which *is* in mount Ephraim, and said, Hear me, thou Jeroboam, and all Israel; [5] Ought ye not to know that the LORD God of Israel gave the kingdom over Israel to David for ever, *even* to him and to his sons by a covenant of salt? 2 Chron 13:4-5 (KJV)

At the time of this writing, the throne of David had already been set up forever. This is a reference to a past event.

> [1] I will sing of the mercies of the LORD for ever: with my mouth will I make known thy faithfulness to all generations. [2] For I have said, Mercy shall be built up for ever: thy faithfulness shalt thou establish in the very heavens.
>
> [3] I have made a covenant with my chosen, I have sworn unto David my servant, [4] Thy seed will I establish for ever, and build up thy throne to all generations. Selah.   [5] And the heavens shall praise thy wonders, O LORD: thy faithfulness also in the congregation of the saints Psalms 89:1-5 (KJV)

Speaking of David in verse 3, God promises to his seed, Solomon, that he will establish his throne to all generations.

> I have found David my servant; with my holy oil have I anointed him: [21] With whom my hand shall be established: mine arm also shall strengthen him. [22] The enemy shall not exact upon him; nor the son of wickedness afflict him. [23] And I will beat down his foes before his face, and plague them that hate him. [24] But my faithfulness and my mercy *shall be* with him: and in my name shall his horn be exalted. [25] I will set his hand also in the sea, and his right hand in the rivers. [26] He shall cry unto me, Thou *art* my father, my God, and the rock of my salvation. [27] Also I will make him *my* firstborn, higher than the kings of the earth.
>
> [28] My mercy will I keep for him for evermore, and my covenant shall stand fast with him. [29] His seed also will I make *to endure* for ever, and his throne as the days of heaven. [30] If his children forsake my law, and walk not in my judgments;
>
> [31] If they break my statutes, and keep not my commandments; [32] Then will I visit their transgression with the rod, and their iniquity with stripes. [33] Nevertheless my lovingkindness will I not utterly take from him, nor suffer my faithfulness to fail.
>
> [34] My covenant will I not break, nor alter the thing that is gone out of my lips. [35] Once have I sworn by my holiness that I will not lie unto David. [36] His seed shall endure for ever, and his throne as the sun before me. [37] It shall be established for ever as the moon, and *as* a faithful witness in heaven. Selah. Psalms 89:20-37 (KJV)

In the above Psalm, we find further confirmation of the continuous and everlasting throne of David. In two other scriptures, God has promised and David has received "the neck of his enemies." David, a man "After God's own heart." Had been protected and prepared for the throne. Here on Earth, it was to be a perpetual throne from generation to generation, and eventually the throne of Christ. (See Luke 1:41-33) In a closer look at Psalm 89, we find confirmation of this.

- He was anointed by God - 89:20.
- The enemy shall not bring harm or affliction - 89:22.
- God himself shall bring down his foes - 89:23.
- God's faithfulness, mercy, and God's name will be with him. - 89: 24.
- I will set his hand in the city - 89:25 (Remember the islands promised to Israel in previously quoted scripture?).
- God's mercy will keep him (his lineage) for evermore, and his covenant will stand fast –89:28.
- David's seed will endure or forever, and his throne as the days of Heaven - 89:29.
- If his children forsake God's laws and walk not in his ways, break his statutes, do not keep his commandments - 89: 30-31.

What happens if the conditions of verses 30 and 31 are not met? Does his throne cease to exist? Can Christ come and sit on David's thrown at his second coming, as stated in Luke 1:31-32, if it does not exist? Not at all! What does happen, if David's heirs do all the bad things listed above?

- He will visit them a with a rod of iron, and with stripes (punishment. Big time) 89:31-32.
- Still he will not break his covenant with David. He will not change his mind, nor will he lie unto David - 89:33-35.
- His seed will endure forever, and his throne will last as long as the sun - 89:36.
- His throne will be established forever, with the moon as a faithful witness in heaven -89:37.

It is very plain; David's throne is to be in continual existence on earth. It will pass through every generation, until Christ assumes the throne.

How can that be? Simply because God said it would be that way. Furthermore, he made provisions for it to come to pass. In spite of sin and rebellion, we can find this unbroken line, both in God's Word and in history. There is undeniable proof.

Call on me and I will show you Great and Mighty things, says a Lord. Jeremiah 33:3

THE MULTI-TASKED PROPHET

Jeremiah was in prison in Jerusalem. His own people put him there for preaching of their coming destruction. This destruction came at the hands of the Chaldeans, while he was there. This message came from God. Jeremiah had been given a commission, some 35 years before. When God called him, the calling was unique, because Jeremiah was very special to God. He was only one of three people in Scripture called and ordained by God for a special task before his birth. The other two are, John the Baptist, and Jesus the Christ. Now, Jeremiah was in prison, and obviously questioning God. He was reflecting back to the enormous commission given him and recorded in Chapter 1. He wondered to himself, if God had broken his promise.

> [1] The words of Jeremiah the son of Hilkiah, of the priests that *were* in Anathoth in the land of Benjamin: [2] To whom the word of the LORD came in the days of Josiah the son of Amon king of Judah, in the thirteenth year of his reign.
>
> [3] It came also in the days of Jehoiakim the son of Josiah king of Judah, unto the end of the eleventh year of Zedekiah the son of Josiah king of Judah, unto the carrying away of Jerusalem captive in the fifth month.
>
> [4] Then the word of the LORD came unto me, saying, [5] Before I formed thee in the belly I knew thee; and before thou camest forth out of the womb I sanctified thee, *and* I ordained thee a prophet unto the nations. [6] Then said I, Ah, Lord GOD! behold, I cannot speak: for I *am* a child. [7] But the LORD said unto me, Say not, I *am* a child: for thou shalt go to all that I shall send thee, and whatsoever I command thee thou shalt speak. [8] Be not afraid of their faces: for I *am* with thee to deliver thee, saith the LORD. [9] Then the LORD put forth his hand, and touched my mouth. And the LORD said unto me, Behold, I have put my words in thy mouth. [10] See, I have this day set thee over the nations and over the

> kingdoms, to root out, and to pull down, and to destroy, and
> to throw down, to build, and to plant. Jer 1:1-10 (KJV)

God's promises to Jeremiah were profound, and his task plainly spelled out.

- God's plan was in effect before the foundation of the world, and Jeremiah was to be a part of it.
- Before Jeremiah was formed in the womb, he was ordained a prophet to the <u>nations</u>. Note here that God says nations. Not a nation, and the nation, or just a Nation of Judah. God had also made sure that Jeremiah's mother was not Pro-choice.
- When God called him, he resisted. He offered an argument, much like Moses did.
- In verse six, paraphrased, he says. "Not me Lord. I'm just a child, and besides, I don't speak very well."
- God told him not to say he was just a child, and he would go where God sent him and he would say what God told him to say (write) – 1:7
- God told him to not be afraid, because He would be with him - 1:8.
- God then touched his mouth and put His own words in his mouth.

Now, Jeremiah was empowered and prepared for the great commission he was to carry out.

> ¹⁰ See, I have this day set thee over the nations and over the kingdoms, to root out, and to pull down, and to destroy, and to throw down, to build, and to plant.

This verse is without question, one of the most significant verses in all of Scripture relating to the prophecy of Judah, Israel, and the birthright nations. Consider the following.

- He is set over nations - more than one.
- He is set over kingdoms, more than one kingdom; there is a difference. A nation does not necessarily have a king, but a kingdom does. The distinction is made clear, as he carries out his commission.
- He is to "root out - pull down - destroying and throw down." Nevertheless, this is only the first part of his commission.
- He is also to build and to plant.
- In these verses, God tells him to:
  o Gird up his loins, arise, and speak as God tells him - 1:7.
  o Go to Jerusalem - 2:2.

Jeremiah followed God's instructions and preached to Judah for approximately 50 years. From the time of Josiah, king of Judah, and the overthrow of Zedekiah and the beginning of the deportation into Babylon in 586 B.C. his message was ignored. Jeremiah was eventually thrown in prison at the instruction of the King of Judah, because he preached against their sins and their coming destruction. This was the time when Jeremiah was questioning his commission from God. He questioned how he could ever complete his task. It seemed impossible, while in a dark, damp dungeon. Especially impossible since he was put there by his very own people.

God spoke to him again. Just at the right time.

[1] In the ninth year of Zedekiah king of Judah, in the tenth month, came Nebuchadrezzar king of Babylon and all his army against Jerusalem, and they besieged it. [2] *And* in the eleventh year of Zedekiah, in the fourth month, the ninth *day* of the month, the city was broken up. [3] And all the princes of the king of Babylon came in, and sat in the

middle gate, *even* Nergalsharezer, Samgarnebo, Sarsechim, Rabsaris, Nergalsharezer, Rabmag, with all the residue of the princes of the king of Babylon.

⁴ And it came to pass, *that* when Zedekiah the king of Judah saw them, and all the men of war, then they fled, and went forth out of the city by night, by the way of the king's garden, by the gate betwixt the two walls: and he went out the way of the plain. ⁵ But the Chaldeans' army pursued after them, and overtook Zedekiah in the plains of Jericho: and when they had taken him, they brought him up to Nebuchadnezzar king of Babylon to Riblah in the land of Hamath, where he gave judgment upon him. ⁶ Then the king of Babylon slew the sons of Zedekiah in Riblah before his eyes: also the king of Babylon slew all the nobles of Judah. ⁷ Moreover he put out Zedekiah's eyes, and bound him with chains, to carry him to Babylon. ⁸ And the Chaldeans burned the king's house, and the houses of the people, with fire, and brake down the walls of Jerusalem. ⁹ Then Nebuzaradan the captain of the guard carried away captive into Babylon the remnant of the people that remained in the city, and those that fell away, that fell to him, with the rest of the people that remained. ¹⁰ But Nebuzaradan the captain of the guard left of the poor of the people, which had nothing, in the land of Judah, and gave them vineyards and fields at the same time.

¹¹ Now Nebuchadrezzar king of Babylon gave charge concerning Jeremiah to Nebuzaradan the captain of the guard, saying, ¹² Take him, and look well to him, and do him no harm; but do unto him even as he shall say unto thee.

¹³ So Nebuzaradan the captain of the guard sent, and Nebushasban, Rabsaris, and Nergalsharezer, Rabmag, and all the king of Babylon's princes; ¹⁴ Even they sent, and took Jeremiah out of the court of the prison, and committed him unto Gedaliah the son of Ahikam the son of Shaphan, that he should carry him home: so he dwelt among the people. ¹⁵ Now the word of the LORD came unto Jeremiah, while he was shut up in the court of the prison, saying, ¹⁶ Go and speak to Ebedmelech the Ethiopian, saying, Thus saith the LORD of hosts, the God of Israel; Behold, I will bring my words upon this city for evil, and not for good; and they shall be *accomplished* in that day before thee. ¹⁷ But I will deliver thee in that day, saith the LORD: and thou shalt not

be given into the hand of the men of whom thou *art* afraid. [18] For I will surely deliver thee, and thou shalt not fall by the sword, but thy life shall be for a prey unto thee: because thou hast put thy trust in me, saith the LORD. Jer 39:1-18 (KJV)

Is this the end of a dynasty? It seems so, but it is not to be. Jeremiah still has to "build and to plant," if God's Word is to be true. We see in these verses that:

- Nebuchadnezzar, king of Babylon, overran the city of Jerusalem, took the king captive, taking him to Riblah -39:5.
- The king of Babylon killed all of Zedekiah's sons and all the nobles of Judah – 39:6
- His intent was to end the dynasty of the Jews once and for all. That idea has repeated itself many times in history, Hitler and Yassir Arafat being the more recent. Now, we have what many would call a "nut case" in Iran who wants to hasten the coming of the "Messiah" by "wiping the Jews off the map."
- Zedekiah was bound in chains, taken to Babylon, and was cast into prison. 39:7

Jeremiah 50 2:11 gives additional information of this event and says that Zedekiah was put in prison "till the day of his death." Indeed Zedekiah died in prison, his heirs had already been killed along with all of the nobles of Judah. It appears that this would be the end of the Throne of David.

- The Chaldeans burned the palace and the homes of all the people, tore down the walls of the city, instituting a "scorched earth" policy - verse 8
- Nebuzaradan, captain of the guard, took all the remaining people except the poor into Babylon as

slaves. The poor remained to attend the vineyards and the field's -verse 9:10

- The king of Babylon gave instructions to Nebuzaradan to free Jeremiah, permit him to be with his people who were left in the land. His freedom now came by the decree of a conquering pagan king. It was a freedom, which he did not enjoy under his own Judean king. Furthermore, he was given food and money to live on. -39:7 - 40:5

In the following three chapters of Jeremiah, we learn that Gedadiah, the son of the governor, was put in charge of all the Jews who remained. God was using the Babylonian rulers to keep this group in the land. Soon, a competitor by the name of Ishmael came to Mizpah. Eventually he killed Gedadiah and took over the small group of Jews. It is here that we find Jeremiah, Baruch, and a new character listed as part of this group. In Jeremiah 41:10, is the first mention of the King's daughters. Their forced departure to the Ammonites is the first time we learn of their existence.

"Oops!"

The Babylonian king Nebuchadrezzar had overlooked something when he put Zedekiah in prison until his death and killed all the royal line of David. He had forgotten about the king's daughters. In his attempt to end David's dynasty, his concern was only with the male heirs. He was unaware of the divine commission and protection given to Jeremiah and all those involved in finishing that commission. Jeremiah would not be finished until he planted and built up as previously instructed.

In 41:11 -- 42, we meet Johanan, captain of the forces who rescued this little party from Ishmael. He brought them back to the town of Chimham, near Bethlehem. Johanan asked for divine advice from God through Jeremiah as to what they should do. He did not know whether they should stay in Judah under the hand of Babylon, or to try and escape to Egypt. Jeremiah prayed to God for advice and was instructed by the Lord to stay in Jerusalem. Furthermore, if they went to Egypt, every one except those under divine protection would die there. However, God's promise and commission was still in effect. Even the rebellion of the small remnant was not going to cancel this mission. Jeremiah relayed God's message to Johanan.

> [1] Then all the captains of the forces, and Johanan the son of Kareah, and Jezaniah the son of Hoshaiah, and all the people from the least even unto the greatest, came near, [2] And said unto Jeremiah the prophet, Let, we beseech thee, our supplication be accepted before thee, and pray for us unto the LORD thy God, *even* for all this remnant; (for we are left *but* a few of many, as thine eyes do behold us:) [3] That the LORD thy God may shew us the way wherein we may walk, and the thing that we may do. [4] Then Jeremiah the prophet said unto them, I have heard *you*; behold, I will pray unto the LORD your God according to your words; and

it shall come to pass, *that* whatsoever thing the LORD shall answer you, I will declare *it* unto you; I will keep nothing back from you. ⁵ Then they said to Jeremiah, The LORD be a true and faithful witness between us, if we do not even according to all things for the which the LORD thy God shall send thee to us. ⁶ Whether *it be* good, or whether *it be* evil, we will obey the voice of the LORD our God, to whom we send thee; that it may be well with us, when we obey the voice of the LORD our God.

⁷ And it came to pass after ten days, that the word of the LORD came unto Jeremiah. ⁸ Then called he Johanan the son of Kareah, and all the captains of the forces which *were* with him, and all the people from the least even to the greatest, ⁹ And said unto them, Thus saith the LORD, the God of Israel, unto whom ye sent me to present your supplication before him; ¹⁰ If ye will still abide in this land, then will I build you, and not pull *you* down, and I will plant you, and not pluck *you* up: for I repent me of the evil that I have done unto you. ¹¹ Be not afraid of the king of Babylon, of whom ye are afraid; be not afraid of him, saith the LORD: for I *am* with you to save you, and to deliver you from his hand. ¹² And I will shew mercies unto you, that he may have mercy upon you, and cause you to return to your own land. ¹³ But if ye say, We will not dwell in this land, neither obey the voice of the LORD your God, ¹⁴ Saying, No; but we will go into the land of Egypt, where we shall see no war, nor hear the sound of the trumpet, nor have hunger of bread; and there will we dwell: ¹⁵ And now therefore hear the word of the LORD, ye remnant of Judah; Thus saith the LORD of hosts, the God of Israel; If ye wholly set your faces to enter into Egypt, and go to sojourn there; ¹⁶ Then it shall come to pass, *that* the sword, which ye feared, shall overtake you there in the land of Egypt, and the famine, whereof ye were afraid, shall follow close after you there in Egypt; and there ye shall die. ¹⁷ So shall it be with all the men that set their faces to go into Egypt to sojourn there; they shall die by the sword, by the famine, and by the pestilence: and none of them shall remain or escape from the evil that I will bring upon them. ¹⁸ For thus saith the LORD of hosts, the God of Israel; As mine anger and my fury hath been poured forth upon the inhabitants of Jerusalem; so shall my fury be poured forth upon you, when ye shall enter into Egypt:

and ye shall be an execration, and an astonishment, and a curse, and a reproach; and ye shall see this place no more. Jer 42:1-18 (KJV)

Jeremiah delivered the Word of God back to the people. However, it was not what they wanted to hear. Even though God warned that if they went to Egypt the very sword they feared would overtake them, they chose not to listen. Denying that the word from Jeremiah was from God, Johanan and the rest of the leaders only wanted to follow God if He agreed with their desires.

> ⁴ So Johanan the son of Kareah, and all the captains of the forces, and all the people, obeyed not the voice of the LORD, to dwell in the land of Judah. ⁵ But Johanan the son of Kareah, and all the captains of the forces, took all the remnant of Judah, that were returned from all nations, whither they had been driven, to dwell in the land of Judah;
>
> ⁶ *Even* men, and women, and children, and the king's daughters, and every person that Nebuzaradan the captain of the guard had left with Gedaliah the son of Ahikam the son of Shaphan, and Jeremiah the prophet, and Baruch the son of Neriah. ⁷ So they came into the land of Egypt: for they obeyed not the voice of the LORD: thus came they *even* to Tahpanhes. Jer 43:4-7 (KJV)

Against God's will, they went to Egypt. Jeremiah, Baruch, and the King's daughters became reluctant travelers. Once in Egypt, the last part of his commission to build up and plant seemed as if it would go unfinished. Once again, Jeremiah was hindered from carrying out God's task, which he was empowered to do. Even still, God's promises and provisions for their safety was in place. After all, Jeremiah was in effect the keeper and transporter of the throne of David. As had been prophesied, the throne had just been " rooted up." Still remaining was the task to plant and build up.

In Jeremiah 44, two entirely different results befall the group in Egypt. The willing travelers and those of Jeremiah's group find different fates await them.

> ²⁴ Moreover Jeremiah said unto all the people, and to all the women, Hear the word of the LORD, all Judah that *are* in the land of Egypt: ²⁵ Thus saith the LORD of hosts, the God of Israel, saying; Ye and your wives have both spoken with your mouths, and fulfilled with your hand, saying, We will surely perform our vows that we have vowed, to burn incense to the queen of heaven, and to pour out drink offerings unto her: ye will surely accomplish your vows, and surely perform your vows. ²⁶ Therefore hear ye the word of the LORD, all Judah that dwell in the land of Egypt; Behold, I have sworn by my great name, saith the LORD, that my name shall no more be named in the mouth of any man of Judah in all the land of Egypt, saying, The Lord GOD liveth. ²⁷ Behold, I will watch over them for evil, and not for good: and all the men of Judah that *are* in the land of Egypt shall be consumed by the sword and by the famine, until there be an end of them. ²⁸ Yet a small number that escape the sword shall return out of the land of Egypt into the land of Judah, and all the remnant of Judah, that are gone into the land of Egypt to sojourn there, shall know whose words shall stand, mine, or theirs. ²⁹ And this *shall be* a sign unto you, saith the LORD, that I will punish you in this place, that ye may know that my words shall surely stand against you for evil: ³⁰ Thus saith the LORD; Behold, I will give Pharaoh Hophra king of Egypt into the hand of his enemies, and into the hand of them that seek his life; as I gave Zedekiah king of Judah into the hand of Nebuchadrezzar king of Babylon, his enemy, and that sought his life. Jer 44:24-30

Once in Egypt, the worship of pagan gods is immediately started. God through Jeremiah again warns of death by the sword and famine. Verse 28 indicates that a small number will return to Judah. This small group is very likely limited to Jeremiah, Baruch, the King's daughters, and a few of the faithful. Chapter 45 confirms Jeremiah's mission that was earlier found in Chapter 1.

¹ The word that Jeremiah the prophet spake unto Baruch the son of Neriah, when he had written these words in a book at the mouth of Jeremiah, in the fourth year of Jehoiakim the son of Josiah king of Judah, saying, ² Thus saith the LORD, the God of Israel, unto thee, O Baruch; ³ Thou didst say, Woe is me now! for the LORD hath added grief to my sorrow; I fainted in my sighing, and I find no rest.

⁴ Thus shalt thou say unto him, The LORD saith thus; Behold, *that* which I have built will I break down, and that which I have planted I will pluck up, even this whole land.

⁵ And seekest thou great things for thyself? seek *them* not: for, behold, I will bring evil upon all flesh, saith the LORD: but thy life will I give unto thee for a prey in all places whither thou goest. Jer 45:1-5 (KJV)

This promise was made during the reign of Jehoiakim, approximately 18 years before the fall of Zedekiah in 587 B.C. The ending of the line of Zedekiah was the Lord's doing. Divine protection was given directly to Baruch as he was directly involved in the task. They were both to be a part of God's tearing down and building up the throne of David.

It would be well to clarify here an enormous truth, too often overlooked by the modern Christian teachers. David's throne (Dynasty) through his seed would continue throughout all generations. Furthermore, the scepter would not depart from Judah. God's promise to David and his son Solomon cannot be overlooked or written off as symbolic. God's Word cannot be ignored. The promise that the throne would never lack a man to sit on it throughout all generations is real. David and Solomon were Kings over all Israel (complete 12 tribes) during their reigns; however, they were the only two kings of the linage of Judah to do so. When Jeroboam took the 10 tribes north, he became the leader and recipient of the promised birthright. David's linage was no longer over all Israel, only over the Tribe of Judah. This continued from the rule of Rehoboam through 19 dynasties until the reign of Zedekiah. This separation of the two kingdoms or nations in no way negates the truth of Scripture.

The promise regarding the continuous line of David's throne was to be through Judah, not a continuous line over the whole house of Israel. The reign over the whole house of Israel will eventually come, but the throne of Israel is to be removed from David's line. It is to be removed from his sons and given to the birthright line for a time. There are a number of scriptures to consider, including Isaiah 11:10-13 and Luke 1:31-33, however for our purposes we will look at First Kings 11: 26-39.

> **26** And Jeroboam the son of Nebat, an Ephrathite of Zereda, Solomon's servant, whose mother's name *was* Zeruah, a widow woman, even he lifted up *his* hand against the king. **27** And this *was* the cause that he lifted up *his* hand against the king: Solomon built Millo, *and* repaired the breaches of the city of David his father.
>
> **28** And the man Jeroboam *was* a mighty man of valour: and Solomon seeing the young man that he was industrious, he made him ruler over all the charge of the house of Joseph. **29** And it came to pass at that time when Jeroboam went out of Jerusalem, that the prophet Ahijah the Shilonite found him in the way; and he had clad himself with a new garment; and they two *were* alone in the field: **30** And Ahijah caught the new garment that *was* on him, and rent it *in* twelve pieces: **31** And he said to Jeroboam, Take thee ten pieces: for thus saith the LORD, the God of Israel, Behold, I will rend the kingdom out of the hand of Solomon, and will give ten tribes to thee: **32** (But he shall have one tribe for my servant David's sake, and for Jerusalem's sake, the city which I have chosen out of all the tribes of Israel:) **33** Because that they have forsaken me, and have worshipped Ashtoreth the goddess of the Zidonians, Chemosh the god of the Moabites, and Milcom the god of the children of Ammon, and have not walked in my ways, to do *that which is* right in mine eyes, and *to keep* my statutes and my judgments, as *did* David his father. **34** Howbeit I will not take the whole kingdom out of his hand: but I will make him prince all the days of his

life for David my servant's sake, whom I chose, because he kept my commandments and my statutes: ³⁵ But I will take the kingdom out of his son's hand, and will give it unto thee, *even* ten tribes. ³⁶ And unto his son will I give one tribe, that David my servant may have a light alway before me in Jerusalem, the city which I have chosen me to put my name there. ³⁷ And I will take thee, and thou shalt reign according to all that thy soul desireth, and shalt be king over Israel. ³⁸ And it shall be, if thou wilt hearken unto all that I command thee, and wilt walk in my ways, and do *that is* right in my sight, to keep my statutes and my commandments, as David my servant did; that I will be with thee, and build thee a sure house, as I built for David, and will give Israel unto thee. ³⁹ And I will for this afflict the seed of David, but not for ever. 1 Kings 11:26-39 (KJV)

The scriptures, quoted earlier, help clarify the continuity of the line of David. They also help us understand the seeming difference we sometimes see between the throne of David and the throne of Israel.

Within this passage, Jeroboam, of the Tribe of Ephraim, (the birthright nation) appears on the scene in verse 26. In verse 29, Jeroboam and the prophet Ahijah are alone in a field. Cutting Jeroboam's coat into 12 pieces, the prophet gave 10 pieces back to Jeroboam and kept the other two. Under God's instructions, the prophet states that Jeroboam is to receive 10 tribes from the hand of Solomon. One piece is then reserved for the line of David, and for the sake of Jerusalem, which had been chosen out of all the tribes of Israel. This word from God is so important that the prophet repeats the instructions of verses 34 thru 37.

One thing is clear, the <u>kingdom</u> is given to Jeroboam, and he is to be king over Israel (verse 37). The promise to Jeroboam, however, was a conditional promise. Jeroboam was to meet the conditions of walking in the way of God, and keeping his commandments. In return, God promised to build him a sure house. We know from both history and Scripture that Jeroboam did not follow God's conditions. Jeroboam and the people immediately fell into idle worship after moving north into Samaria. How does Scripture reconcile these seemingly contradictory promises?

Returning to the plight of Jeremiah and those with him, they are back in Judah as subjects of the King of Babylon. There they were granted limited freedom, including travel. The freedom of travel is important to God's plans for them. God used a pagan king to ensure that Jeremiah and his company were granted this "passport." As we shall see, it was well used.

Before investigating Jeremiah's travels and traveling companions, another important character needs an introduction. Jeconiah was the son of Jehoiakim, and ruled in Jerusalem for three 3 months and 10 days. At that point, he was replaced by the vassal king Zedekiah by Nebuchadnezzar. You may recall that Jehoiakim was exiled to Babylon and put into prison. Later, he was appointed king by the evil Merodac. (See 1 Chronicles 3:16; Jeremiah 20 4:1; 2 Kings 25:27-30; and Jeremiah 52: 31-34 for background) Jeremiah uses the name Coniah when speaking of Jeconiah (Jeremiah 22:1 and 37:1; 1 Chronicles 3:16). Much is said about this short-term king, and it seemed as if he would continue the throne of David. However, it was not to be. Why? Simply because God said so:

> [24] As I live, saith the LORD, though Coniah the son of Jehoiakim king of Judah were the signet upon my right hand, yet would I pluck thee thence; [25] And I will give thee into the hand of them that seek thy life, and into the hand *of them* whose face thou fearest, even into the hand of Nebuchadrezzar king of Babylon, and into the hand of the Chaldeans.

²⁶ And I will cast thee out, and thy mother that bare thee, into another country, where ye were not born; and there shall ye die. ²⁷ But to the land whereunto they desire to return, thither shall they not return.

²⁸ *Is* this man Coniah a despised broken idol? *is he* a vessel wherein *is* no pleasure? wherefore are they cast out, he and his seed, and are cast into a land which they know not? ²⁹ O earth, earth, earth, hear the word of the LORD. ³⁰ Thus saith the LORD, Write ye this man childless, a man *that* shall not prosper in his days: for no man of his seed shall prosper, sitting upon the throne of David, and ruling any more in Judah.   Jer 22:24-30 (KJV)

In verse 30, God proclaimed that Coniah would be childless. At this point Coniah's lineage would no longer prosper nor sit on the throne of David in Judah. The matter had been ended by God.

In summary:

- Nebuchadrezzar had attempted to destroy completely the true linage to the throne of David
- He overlooked the king's daughters, considering them unimportant since they were normally not considered qualified to sit on the throne or continue the linage
- God had other plans, through his strange commission to Jeremiah, he was to "build and to plant"
- This commission was not yet complete with the Babylonian exile
- Jeremiah, the King's daughters, and Baruch were forced to travel to Egypt
- God promised them protection and that they would escape Egypt and return to their own land

- In verse 28 of chapter 44, God repeated these assurances to Jeremiah and his companions

- They are to escape and return to Judah would further prove God's Words to be true
- In the 45:2-5, Baruch was assured that he too was under divine protection

Even men, and women, and children, and the king's daughters, and every person that Nebuzaradan the captain of the guard had left with Gedaliah the son of Ahikam the son of Shaphan, and Jeremiah the prophet, and Baruch the son of Neriah. 7 So they came into the land of Egypt: for they obeyed not the voice of the LORD: thus came they even to Tahpanhes. Jer 43:6-7 (KJV)	14 So that none of the remnant of Judah, which are gone into the land of Egypt to sojourn there, shall escape or remain, that they should return into the land of Judah, to the which they have a desire to return to dwell there: for none shall return but such as shall escape. Jer 44:14 (KJV)

As Jeremiah returned from Egypt, on his trek through the land of Judah, God gave him the words of warning to speak to the Gentile nations surrounding Israel. This is recorded in chapters 46 thru 51. Chapter 52 then recaps the fall of Jerusalem previously recorded in chapter 39. The matter of Zedekiah's death in prison is recorded here. When Jeremiah returned to Judah, concluding his series of warnings, there is no further reference to him in the book bearing his name. Many assume he dies here, or simply fades away becoming insignificant. However, there are secular, historical writings that report a continued journey for Jeremiah. These writings are very interesting when we consider the last part of God's commission to Jeremiah. Remaining for Jeremiah was a task to, "build up and to plant," in order to fulfill his commission. The question we must ask ourselves is this, "is God's Word true when he gives Jeremiah this commission?" If the answer is "yes," then we must search history to find the answer.

In the Mouth of Two Witnesses

In Deuteronomy 17:6 and in 19:5, a principle is established that two or more witnesses must agree before the truth of a matter can be verified. In other words, in the mouth of two or more witnesses, something can be accepted as true. Paul reiterates this in second Corinthians 13:1. (*This is the third time I am coming to you. In the mouth of two or three witnesses shall every word be established.* 2 Cor 13:1) Amos 3:7 also confirms this principle by using the words servant and prophet in the plural. (*Surely the Lord GOD will do nothing, but he revealeth his secret unto his servants the prophets.* Amos 3:7)

In the light of these scriptures, we should be able to confirm the carrying out of Jeremiah's commission in at least one other place in Scripture. So to be consistent with Scripture we look for at least one other place where God has, "revealed his secrets to his servants the prophets."

A Riddle and a Parable

Such a confirmation can be found in Ezekiel 17:1-24. The events of the fall of Judah and the planting of the throne of David are described here. This is done in the form of a riddle, however God himself explains the riddle in sharp detail.

> [1] And the word of the LORD came unto me, saying, [2] Son of man, put forth a riddle, and speak a parable unto the house of Israel; [3] And say, Thus saith the Lord GOD; A great eagle with great wings, longwinged, full of feathers, which had divers colours, came unto Lebanon, and took the highest branch of the cedar: [4] He cropped off the top of his young twigs, and carried it into a land of traffick; he set it in a city

of merchants. ⁵ He took also of the seed of the land, and planted it in a fruitful field; he placed *it* by great waters, *and* set it *as* a willow tree. ⁶ And it grew, and became a spreading vine of low stature, whose branches turned toward him, and the roots thereof were under him: so it became a vine, and brought forth branches, and shot forth sprigs. ⁷ There was also another great eagle with great wings and many feathers: and, behold, this vine did bend her roots toward him, and shot forth her branches toward him, that he might water it by the furrows of her plantation.

⁸ It was planted in a good soil by great waters, that it might bring forth branches, and that it might bear fruit, that it might be a goodly vine. ⁹ Say thou, Thus saith the Lord GOD; Shall it prosper? shall he not pull up the roots thereof, and cut off the fruit thereof, that it wither? it shall wither in all the leaves of her spring, even without great power or many people to pluck it up by the roots thereof. ¹⁰ Yea, behold, *being* planted, shall it prosper? shall it not utterly wither, when the east wind toucheth it? it shall wither in the furrows where it grew. ¹¹ Moreover the word of the LORD came unto me, saying, ¹² Say now to the rebellious house, Know ye not what these *things mean?* tell *them,* Behold, the king of Babylon is come to Jerusalem, and hath taken the king thereof, and the princes thereof, and led them with him to Babylon; ¹³ And hath taken of the king's seed, and made a covenant with him, and hath taken an oath of him: he hath also taken the mighty of the land: ¹⁴ That the kingdom might be base, that it might not lift itself up, *but* that by keeping of his covenant it might stand. ¹⁵ But he rebelled against him in sending his ambassadors into Egypt, that they might give him horses and much people. Shall he prosper? shall he escape that doeth such *things?* or shall he break the covenant, and be delivered? ¹⁶ *As* I live, saith the Lord GOD, surely in the place *where* the king *dwelleth* that made him king, whose oath he despised, and whose covenant he brake, *even* with him in the midst of Babylon he shall die. ¹⁷ Neither shall Pharaoh with *his* mighty army and great company make for him in the war, by casting up mounts, and building forts, to cut off many persons: ¹⁸ Seeing he despised the oath by breaking the covenant, when, lo, he had given his hand, and hath done all these *things,* he shall not escape. ¹⁹ Therefore thus saith the Lord

GOD; *As* I live, surely mine oath that he hath despised, and my covenant that he hath broken, even it will I recompense upon his own head. ²⁰ And I will spread my net upon him, and he shall be taken in my snare, and I will bring him to Babylon, and will plead with him there for his trespass that he hath trespassed against me. ²¹ And all his fugitives with all his bands shall fall by the sword, and they that remain shall be scattered toward all winds: and ye shall know that I the LORD have spoken *it*.

²² Thus saith the Lord GOD; I will also take of the highest branch of the high cedar, and will set *it*; I will crop off from the top of his young twigs a tender one, and will plant *it* upon an high mountain and eminent: ²³ In the mountain of the height of Israel will I plant it: and it shall bring forth boughs, and bear fruit, and be a goodly cedar: and under it shall dwell all fowl of every wing; in the shadow of the branches thereof shall they dwell. ²⁴ And all the trees of the field shall know that I the LORD have brought down the high tree, have exalted the low tree, have dried up the green tree, and have made the dry tree to flourish: I the LORD have spoken and have done *it*.   Ezek 17:1-24 (KJV)

In this riddle and parable, God told Ezekiel to speak unto the house of Israel and all of God's people. At this time, the Kingdom of Israel had already gone north and had been disbursed by the Assyrians in 721 B.C. Ezekiel was writing in approximately 600 B.C., or about 120 years after the event. Therefore the words to the house of Israel are all encompassing and for a distant future. The more specific details of the riddle however, contained in 17:4 & 11-24, are directed toward Judah. Within these verses, God outlines the exact sequence of events described in Jeremiah regarding the overthrow and replanting of the Scepter Line and Throne of David back into the Throne of and Kingdom of Israel.

- The great eagle in the verse 12 is explained by God as being Nebuchadrezzar who took the king and princes of Jerusalem into Babylon (nothing about the princesses)

- The seed of the land in verses 5 and 6 is explained in verses 13-15 as the people of the land
  - ○ Some he took to Babylon
  - ○ Others were left in Judah to tend to the land
  - ○ Some obeyed and some rebelled as detailed in Jeremiah 42-44
- Those who rebelled went into Egypt and died in a later conflict between Egypt and Babylon
- The remnant whom God promised to save (Jeremiah, Baruch, the King's daughters, and their small entourage) were saved and escaped
- *²² Thus saith the Lord GOD; I will also take of the highest branch of the high cedar, and will set it; I will crop off from the top of his young twigs a tender one, and will plant it upon an high mountain and eminent:*
  - ○ God says he will take of the highest cedar -King Zedekiah
  - ○ You will take of his young twigs (plural)
  - ○ And will take a tender one (singular) and plant it upon a high mountain
  - ○ And (she) will be eminent
- In God's explanation of riddle, he tells Ezekiel he will plant it in the mountain of the height of Israel, not Judah. It is the lineage of Judah that he is planting
- At the time of the planting, the scepter line and the birthright line are partially united
  - ○ A third confirmation of this truth is found in Isaiah 37:41. In this brief verse Isaiah confirms the second half of Jeremiah's commission along with the riddle and parable found in Ezekiel 17

- *³¹ And the remnant that is escaped of the house of Judah shall again take root downward, and bear fruit upward: Isaiah 37:31 (KJV)*

- o Oh the glory and the accuracy of God's Word
- ▪ In verse 24, of Ezek 17 God says "all the trees of the field" meaning the entire world – (see Matthew 13:48), so says the Son of God. He has brought down the high tree (Zedekiah) of the Perez line and exalted the low tree (the line of Zarah). They will carry on the lineage of David and bring it back into a place of exaltation. The low tree will flourish.

There is much more that could be said regarding the two lines of Judah, (Perez and Zarah,) but space will not permit dealing with that at this time. The main point is that this is an amazing confirmation of exactly what took place in the fall of Judah and the fulfilling of the second half of Jeremiah's commission to "build and to plant" in the book bearing his name.

On the Road Again

We find Jeremiah, Baruch his scribe, and the king's daughter in Egypt but under the divine protection of God's promise to escape. He has yet some dire warnings to give to gentile nations, beginning in chapter 46. These include Egypt, the Philistines, Moab, the Ammonites, and the Babylonians. Those warnings are to cover centuries of time. However, through these prophecies of destruction God still reminds Jeremiah that he is under His divine protection.

Jeremiah now travels north and west, by foot and by boat with his precious cargo; as we will see later both his route and his destination. It is safe to say, he is divinely driven by the last half of his commission from God (Jeremiah 1: 10), "to build and plant," and **that he** must do. His precious cargo was vital to all the promises God made to Abraham, Isaac, Jacob, and Joseph. Through them are promises to the nations of the world and the resulting blessings.

The king's daughter whose names were "Scata" and "Tamar Tephi", were his great grand daughters (King Zedekiah was Jeremiah's grandson) and he knew he must "plant" this royal line that would fulfill the prophecy in Isaiah 37:31. *And the remnant that is escaped of the house of Judah shall again take root downward, and bear fruit upward..* This was in full accordance with God's law as recorded in Numbers 27:8 *And thou shalt speak unto the children of Israel, saying, If a man die, and have no son, then ye shall cause his inheritance to pass unto his daughter.* God further reminded Jeremiah in 18:7 that He would pluck up, pull down and destroy a nation. In verse 9, he added that He would also build and plant.

We find that the soil had already been prepared for the building up and planting by some of the tribes of

Judah and Israel (Ephraim) in a new land. In the <u>History of Ireland</u>,[18] written by Geoffrey Keating, he writes that a Hebrew name Parthalon settles in the land now known as Ireland and established a kingdom there. The exact date is in question, but it was long before Jeremiah's arrival. Tuatha de Danaan (Tribe of Dan) arrived in Ireland in two different contingencies during or near the end of the reign of David, King of Israel (approximately 1015 BC).

A reference to the Dannites migration north and west is recorded in Judges 5:17. Another Hebrew tribe, a descendent of Eber the Hebrew, merged with the Dannites. Eventually a capital was set up at what is now Tara, having the name changed several times in the process. During all these migrations and invasions, a detailed record of all the kings, and the dates of the reign, was maintained. This is recorded in Keating's <u>History of Ireland</u>.

In Genesis 40 9:17, Dan is called a "serpent by the way", indicating a crooked path that he would travel. Another previously referred to characteristic was that he was a warrior-conqueror. Each town or village he conquered he renamed after his father Dan. See Judges 18: 27-29 and Joshua 19:47. This characteristic continued for centuries and reflects their culture even today. Remember, in the Hebrew written language, there are no vowels. When a vowel is added: it can be any of the standard vowels, a – e – I – o – u, to form Da, De, Di, Do, or Du. There is no doubt that God intends for us to be able to trace the outpouring of His blessings to the Birthright Nations. The 2006 National Geographic map of Ireland shows at least 199 towns and villages that begin with the letter "D," indicating a direct influence of the Tribe of Dan. There are also many lakes and rivers bearing the name "Dan".

---

[18] Keating, Geoffrey. *History of Ireland.* Translated by John O'Mahony. New York: P.M. Haverty, 1857 [Electronic Version: Google Books]

ENTER JEREMIAH

In the "History of Egypt[19]", Sir Flindrs Petrie presents a detailed account of Jeremiah and his entourage. In 582 B.C., the early records tell of a ship called the Iberian Dannan (remember Dan was in ships Judges 5:19) was shipwrecked off the north east coast of Ireland at Carrickfergus. Its cargo was a man referred to as "Ollamh Fodhla", meaning Holy Seer or Prophet. He was accompanied by his servant, "Bruch". Most importantly, on the ship was a royal princess and in her possession was a chest and their history tells of a stone called, "Lia Fail", meaning the wonderful stone, which was highly treasured and protected at their own peril. This same stone is now believed to be the Coronation Stone of England, in use for centuries. More on that in the chapter on England's Coronation Chair. The records include another amazing event; the royal princess, the daughter of Zedekiah of the royal line of Perez married Eschaidh the Heremon, King of Ireland. He was of the royal line of Zarah, the twin son of Judah. This marriage healed the breach as described at their birth and recorded in Genesis 38: 27-30 (see especially verse 29). This also fulfilled the prophecy found in Ezekiel 21: 26-27 Re: the overturn of the Kingdom of Judah. This royal princess now became the royal Queen Tamar Tephi" and was fully qualified to fulfill another of Ezekiel's prophecy of the tender twig being planted on a high mountain (kingdom) and eminent.

> [18] Seeing he despised the oath by breaking the covenant, when, lo, he had given his hand, and hath done all these *things*, he shall not escape. [19] Therefore thus saith the Lord GOD; *As* I live, surely mine oath that he hath despised, and my covenant that he hath broken, even it will I recompense upon his own head. [20] And I will spread my net upon him,

---

[19] Flinders, Petrie W. M. *A History of Egypt*. [Electronic Version] us.archive.org

and he shall be taken in my snare, and I will bring him to Babylon, and will plead with him there for his trespass that he hath trespassed against me. [21] And all his fugitives with all his bands shall fall by the sword, and they that remain shall be scattered toward all winds: and ye shall know that I the LORD have spoken *it*.

[22] Thus saith the Lord GOD; I will also take of the highest branch of the high cedar, and will set *it*; I will crop off from the top of his young twigs a tender one, and will plant *it* upon an high mountain and eminent: [23] In the mountain of the height of Israel will I plant it: and it shall bring forth boughs, and bear fruit, and be a goodly cedar: and under it shall dwell all fowl of every wing; in the shadow of the branches thereof shall they dwell. [24] And all the trees of the field shall know that I the LORD have brought down the high tree, have exalted the low tree, have dried up the green tree, and have made the dry tree to flourish: I the LORD have spoken and have done *it*.   Ezek 17:18-24 (KJV)

Note in 17:24, God says that He has brought down the high tree (Perez line) and exalted the low tree. Since Zarah, who was really the first-born, the "breach" of Genesis 38 was healed and recorded the second time.

God says to the wicked king of Judah, Zedekiah, that he will remove the diadem (the coronation Stone), and the crown. He will exalt him that which is low (Zarah line) and abase him that is high (Pheraz line). In verse 27 God promises to overturn three times until this kingdom, the crown and proper credentials settles into a place where the rightful owner (Christ) will receive it. Remember, in Psalms 89, God says to David that he will not break His covenant with him. *His seed shall endure forever, and his throne as the sun before me. [37] It shall be established forever as the moon, and as a faithful witness in heaven. Selah.* Psalms 89:36-37 (KJV)

The First Overturn

Jeremiah and the king's daughter took the stone and the bloodline to Ireland in 583 BC. The princess married the king of Ireland (Eochodh also spelled Eschaidh) of the line of Zarah thus reuniting the royal lion of Judah.

Second Overturn

The stone stayed in Ireland for over 10 centuries. Wars and conflicts caused it to be removed, by Fargus, along with the royal line to Scotland in 503A.D. The record of this is found in the "History of Ireland", written by Geoffrey Keating.

Third Overturn

England conquered Scotland and in 1296 A.D. Edward I moved the stone and crown to England. For the past 700 years, the royal line has been crowned over Jacobs Pillar, now known as the Coronation Stone.

Of specific interest, is God's use of the word overturn three times. Upon its arrival in England, the stone representing the Throne of the Line of Judah, had been moved three times. Ezekiel's prophecy had been fulfilled. Israel and Judah began to unite in a small way. The unification will not be complete until the return of Christ to set on the Throne of David forever. Other chapters establish many Old Testament Prophecies, as well as the Apostle Paul's, confirmation of this truth. However, in 1996, the stone was permitted to be moved back to Scotland for security reasons. The <u>throne</u>, meanwhile, remains in England.

The Queen of England is a direct descendent of the Zarah/Perez line. This is in the fulfillment of the prophecy of Nathan speak to King David in 2 Samuel 7:10-17. In that prophetic promise, David is to have a direct Blood Line descendent ruling over his people forever. Psalm 89 confirms further this would be true as long as the sun and moon are in the sky. I believe Biblical and historical evidence confirms that the Line of David is firmly established in England to this present day

Now another great Bible truths is in place. The Scepter Line (Judah) is now in the same country that fulfilled the promise made to Joseph's youngest son Ephraim, the joint recipient of the Birthright along with Manasseh. Manasseh's "great nation" Birthright is yet to be completly accomplished when Ephraim "spills over the wall".[20] This placement of the Scepter Line of Judah in the Birthright nation was only a partial reuniting of the nations Juda and Israel. The complete reuniting of the whole house of Israel only takes place at the return of Christ and he takes the throne of David "until whose right it is" Ezekiel 21:27b. However, it shall be overturned no more, so says the Word of God.

Examine the two charts on the next pages. They offer interesting insight to the Royal Lineage of Britain.

---

[20] See Genesis 49:22

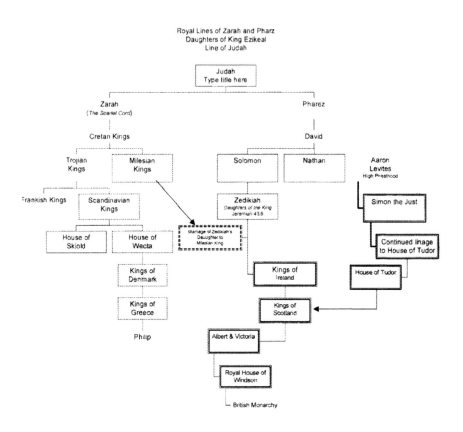

Royal Lines of Zarah and Pharz
Daughters of King Ezikeal
Line of Judah

** Timeline created by Dr. William Class for this publication

Time Line of the Movement
Of Jacob's Pillar
(To the time of becoming the Coronation Stone of England)

Jacob's Dream	1930 BC
Rock taken to Egypt	1883 BC
Period of the Exodus	1453 BC
Into Canaan Territory	1413 BC
At Shechem with Joshua	1383 BC
Abimelech crowned by Pillar	1150 BC
Rehboam Crowned	931 BC
Joash Crowned	798 BC
Stone to Jerusalem	Date Unknown
Josiah's Covenant by Pillar	640 BC
With Jeremiah to Ireland	583 BC
Fergus moves stone to Scotland	500 AD
Edward I takes Stone to England	1296 AD

~~Please note that dates are subject to discussion and to be taken as approximate based on Biblical and Historical evidence.**Scriptural references used to establish the above events are: Genesis 28:10-ff & 49:24; Numbers 14:33; Joshua 24:24-ff; Judges 9:1 & 6; 1 Kings 12:1; 2 Kings 11:13-ff; & 2 Kings 23:3.

THE HISTORY OF "THE ROCK"

Jacob's Pillow

We will now detail further the history of Jacob's Pillow, later referred to simply as "Pillar." Of significance is to understand what it meant to the people of Israel and most importantly to the Throne of David.

> [10] And Jacob went out from Beersheba, and went toward Haran. [11] And he lighted upon a certain place, and tarried there all night, because the sun was set; and he took of the stones of that place, and put *them for* his pillows, and lay down in that place to sleep.
>
> [12] And he dreamed, and behold a ladder set up on the earth, and the top of it reached to heaven: and behold the angels of God ascending and descending on it. [13] And, behold, the LORD stood above it, and said, I *am* the LORD God of Abraham thy father, and the God of Isaac: the land whereon thou liest, to thee will I give it, and to thy seed; [14] And thy seed shall be as the dust of the earth, and thou shalt spread abroad to the west, and to the east, and to the north, and to the south: and in thee and in thy seed shall all the families of the earth be blessed. [15] And, behold, I *am* with thee, and will keep thee in all *places* whither thou goest, and will bring thee again into this land; for I will not leave thee, until I have done *that* which I have spoken to thee of.

16 And Jacob awaked out of his sleep, and he said, Surely the LORD is in this place; and I knew *it* not. **17** And he was afraid, and said, How dreadful *is* this place! this *is* none other but the house of God, and this *is* the gate of heaven. **18** And Jacob rose up early in the morning, and took the stone that he had put *for* his pillows, and set it up *for* a pillar, and poured oil upon the top of it. **19** And he called the name of that place Bethel: but the name of that city *was called* Luz at the first. **20** And Jacob vowed a vow, saying, If God will be with me, and will keep me in this way that I go, and will give me bread to eat, and raiment to put on,

21 So that I come again to my father's house in peace; then shall the LORD be my God: **22** And this stone, which I have set *for* a pillar, shall be God's house: and of all that thou shalt give me I will surely give the tenth unto thee. *Gen 28:10-22 (KJV)*

In Gen. 23, Isaac sent Jacob away to obtain a wife and reaffirmed God's blessing that had come directly from God to Abraham to Isaac now upon Jacob– vs. 1 – 4

Jacob came to a city called Luz and rested for the night. There he took a stone for a pillow and went to sleep. While sleeping the Lord spoke to him and further confirmed His blessings – vs. 13 – 15

When Jacob awoke, he said, "This is none other but the house of God and this is the gate of heaven" – v. 17

He took the stone that he had used for a pillow and anointed it for a witness and renamed the place Beth-el, meaning The House of God – vs. 18 – 19

In Genesis 31:13, God declared that He is the God of Beth-el and accepts the anointing of the stone, performed by Jacob at Beth-el

9 And God appeared unto Jacob again, when he came out of Padanaram, and blessed him. **10** And God said unto him,

Thy name is Jacob: thy name shall not be called any more Jacob, but Israel shall be thy name: and he called his name Israel. **¹¹** And God said unto him, I am God Almighty: be fruitful and multiply; a nation and a company of nations shall be of thee, and kings shall come out of thy loins; **¹²** And the land which I gave Abraham and Isaac, to thee I will give it, and to thy seed after thee will I give the land. **¹³** And God went up from him in the place where he talked with him. **¹⁴** And Jacob set up a pillar in the place where he talked with him, even a pillar of stone: and he poured a drink offering thereon, and he poured oil thereon. **¹⁵** And Jacob called the name of the place where God spake with him, Bethel. *Gen 35:9-15 (KJV)*

God appeared to Jacob again changing his name to Israel and again confirmed His blessing – vs. 10 - 13

Jacob set up a pillar and again anointed it with oil – vs. 11 – 14

The Rock – the Next Generation

²² Joseph is a fruitful bough, even a fruitful bough by a well; whose branches run over the wall: **²³** The archers have sorely grieved him, and shot at him, and hated him: **²⁴** But his bow abode in strength, and the arms of his hands were made strong by the hands of the mighty God of Jacob; (from thence is the shepherd, the stone of Israel:) **²⁵** Even by the God of thy father, who shall help thee; and by the Almighty, who shall bless thee with blessings of heaven above, blessings of the deep that lieth under, blessings of the breasts, and of the womb: **²⁶** The blessings of thy father have prevailed above the blessings of my progenitors unto the utmost bound of the everlasting hills: they shall be on the head of Joseph, and on the crown of the head of him that was separate from his brethren. *Gen 49:22-26 (KJV)*

In Genesis 49, Jacob is on his deathbed, passing on God's blessings to his sons. The material blessings are passed to Joseph as recorded in an earlier chapter. At this pivotal point, Jacob separates the Spiritual and Material blessings. These separate blessings he pronounces on just two of the twelve sons. The material blessings he bestows upon Joseph beginning in verse 22, the important action taking place in verse 24. God, through Jacob, says that his (Jacob's) bow and the arms of his hands were made strong by the hands of the mighty God of Jacob. To paraphrase, from the mighty hands of God comes the Shepard (Christ also called the Rock in 1 Cor. 10:4) and the Stone of Israel (Jacob) has now transferred to Joseph.

Following scripture, the rock is next encountered in the Wilderness of Sin with Moses. A thirsty and disgruntled band, approximately four and a half million Israelites, demand that Moses provide drink. Moses cried to the Lord for help.

> ¹ And all the congregation of the children of Israel journeyed from the wilderness of Sin, after their journeys, according to the commandment of the LORD, and pitched in Rephidim: and *there was* no water for the people to drink. ² Wherefore the people did chide with Moses, and said, Give us water that we may drink. And Moses said unto them, Why chide ye with me? wherefore do ye tempt the LORD? ³ And the people thirsted there for water; and the people murmured against Moses, and said, Wherefore *is* this *that* thou hast brought us up out of Egypt, to kill us and our children and our cattle with thirst?
>
> ⁴ And Moses cried unto the LORD, saying, What shall I do unto this people? they be almost ready to stone me. ⁵ And the LORD said unto Moses, Go on before the people, and take with thee of the elders of Israel; and thy rod, wherewith thou smotest the river, take in thine hand, and go. ⁶ Behold, I will stand before thee there upon the rock in Horeb; and thou shalt smite the rock, and there shall come water out of it, that the people may drink. And Moses did so in the sight of the elders of Israel. *Ex 17:1-6 (KJV)*

Notice that this is not just any rock found along the way. It is described using the definite article, "the". God will stand on "the rock", and Moses will smite "the rock". Same rock, same God, and blessings flow from the rock. A similar instance of the rock giving water is found in Numbers 20:1-13. This time Moses is instructed simply to speak to the rock, however, in his anger he struck the rock twice causing God to discipline him for a lack of faith. It is noteworthy to mention here that when the Children of Israel were preparing to leave Egypt, the preparation for the Exodus did not include carrying drinking water. From this point, Moses displays a greater trust in God to provide drinking water as demonstrated in Numbers 20 and 21 when preparing to move the congregation through occupied lands.

> [17] Let us pass, I pray thee, through thy country: we will not pass through the fields, or through the vineyards, neither will we drink *of* the water of the wells: we will go by the king's *high* way, we will not turn to the right hand nor to the left, until we have passed thy borders. Num 20:17 (KJV)
>
> [21] And Israel sent messengers unto Sihon king of the Amorites, saying, [22] Let me pass through thy land: we will not turn into the fields, or into the vineyards; we will not drink *of* the waters of the well: *but* we will go along by the king's *high* way, until we be past thy borders.
>
> Num 21:21-22 (KJV)

While neither the Amorites nor the Edomites granted the request of Moses, the events stand to show the trust Moses had learned to have in God's ability to provide water.

Next, we see the Stone in Schechem. It is set up by Joshua as a witness to keep the people from breaking their promise to obey God, as they were about to enter the Promised Land.

²⁴ And the people said unto Joshua, The LORD our God will we serve, and his voice will we obey.

²⁵ So Joshua made a covenant with the people that day, and set them a statute and an ordinance in Shechem. ²⁶ And Joshua wrote these words in the book of the law of God, and took a great stone, and set it up there under an oak, that *was* by the sanctuary of the LORD. ²⁷ And Joshua said unto all the people, Behold, this stone shall be a witness unto us; for it hath heard all the words of the LORD which he spake unto us: it shall be therefore a witness unto you, lest ye deny your God. *Josh 24:24-27 (KJV)*

The Rock, later seen as a symbol of the Kingship of Israel and of Christ, began with Jacob's Beth-el (House of God) stone. There are many more references in scripture to the Rock. Below is a representative listing of such passages.

- Deut. 32
  - V. 4 – God is the Rock
  - Vs. 8 & 15 – The Rock is the salvation of the Children of Israel
  - Vs. 17-18 – The Rock begat those who had forgotten him
- Ps. 81:16 – Honey and water from the Rock
- Ps. 105:41 – "opened the Rock"
- Is. 48:21 – God caused water to come out of the Rock and "clave" (spit) the Rock
- 1 Cor. 10:4 – "And did all drink the same spiritual drink: for they drank of that spiritual Rock that followed them: and that Rock was Christ"

Two things become very apparent in these verses. First, the Rock went with the Children of Israel throughout their journeys and history. (Notice in the picture on pages 132 and 138, the rope holes that are worn into the stone, indicating the Rock was transported with the people as they moved) Second, the Rock is a symbol of the coming Messiah (Scepter line).

In Judges 9:1-6, Abimelech is crowned king by the "pillar". *And all the men of Shechem gathered together, and all the house of Millo, and went, and made Abimelech king, by the plain of the pillar that was in Shechem.* (Judges 9:6 (KJV)) The "pillow of Jacob" has for the Israelites become a "pillar" of stone set up in the plain as a symbol of power and kingship.

Hosea 3:4-5[21] contains many pearls of wisdom and will be discussed in detail in a later chapter. For now, focus on verse 4 as it applies to the subject of the stone. In this instance the Holman Christian Standard Bible (HCSB) is used for better understanding. The KJV translates "sacred pillar" as "image". The Hebrew, "***matstsebah*** — NASB Greek-Hebrew Dictionary", is used here, normally rendered pillar. (Strong's #663 a) This translation (pillar) is also used by the New King James Version, the American Standard Bible, American Standard Version, and others. The events described in Hosea 3:4 mirror exactly what happened when Assyria overran Samaria and took Israel (not Juda) captive.

1. "Many days without king" - As previously considered,

---

[21] [4] For the Israelites must live many days without king or prince, without sacrifice or sacred pillar, and without ephod or household idols. Hosea 3:4 (HCSB)

Jeroboam the Ephrathite was made King (1 Kings 11)

2. "Without a sacrifice" – False sacrifices and false Gods were adopted immediately upon going north to Samaria
3. They remained in pagan worship until the Assyrians took them captive in 721 BC.
4. The sacred pillow (see image) referred to here remained with Solomon's line (scepter line as we see later) for the sake of David – 1 Kings 11

However, Jeroboam was their king, and they were known as the Kingdom of Israel until the captivity by the Assyrians.

> ¹ And it came to pass, when Solomon had finished the building of the house of the LORD, and the king's house, and all Solomon's desire which he was pleased to do, ² That the LORD appeared to Solomon the second time, as he had appeared unto him at Gibeon. ³ And the LORD said unto him, I have heard thy prayer and thy supplication, that thou hast made before me: I have hallowed this house, which thou hast built, to put my name there for ever; and mine eyes and mine heart shall be there perpetually.
>
> ⁴ And if thou wilt walk before me, as David thy father walked, in integrity of heart, and in uprightness, to do according to all that I have commanded thee, *and* wilt keep my statutes and my judgments: ⁵ Then I will establish the throne of thy kingdom upon Israel for ever, as I promised to David thy father, saying, There shall not fail thee a man upon the throne of Israel. ⁶ *But* if ye shall at all turn from following me, ye or your children, and will not keep my commandments *and* my statutes which I have set before you, but go and serve other gods, and worship them: ⁷ Then will I cut off Israel out of the land which I have given them; and this house, which I have hallowed for my name, will I cast out of my sight; and Israel shall be a proverb and a byword among all people: ⁸ And at this house, *which* is high, every one that passeth by it shall be astonished, and shall hiss; and they shall say, Why hath the LORD done thus unto this land, and to this house?   *1 Kings 9:1-8 (KJV)*

In God's covenant with Solomon, the restriction of obedience to God's commandments, especially serving him only, are laid out plainly. The requirement of obedience applies to Solomon and his children. The penalty for disobedience, however, falls upon all of Israel. God is addressing the Kingdom of Israel, which included Judah at the time. Hosea 3:4 gives us a picture of the result of such disobedience. Israel "shall abide many days without a king." Keep in mind that the "Kingdom of Israel" and the "Throne of David" are two distinct things. The Throne of David and Kingdom of Israel were described in pages 83 &95.

Ireland's Rich History

If Jeremiah arrived in Ireland in 583 B.C. along with the princess Tamar Tephi who was soon to become queen, and if this dynasty stayed in Ireland for about 900 years we can expect that both Jeremiah and the Queen died there. Ireland is replete with such evidence. On the Devenish Island, you can find Jeremiah's tomb carved out of solid rock, a fitting resting place for such a man of God. The tomb is sealed by a giant stone carved in the shape of a large throne.

In the County of Meath is Tara, the place where Queen Tamar Tephi was buried. Legend records that she requested the great chest brought by her from Jerusalem be buried with here. It is believed to contain the two documents of evidence of ownership and the right of redemption recorded in Jeremiah 32. This is the evidence of Jeremiah's purchase of a field. Such evidence was to be "placed in an earthen vessel, that it may continue many days." Her tomb is believed, by some, to contain the Ark of the Covenant, and was the subject of the popular movie the "Raiders of the Lost Ark".

Her tomb, or "barrow" is the only ancient tomb in the town that has not been excavated. Ruling authorities will not permit excavations, although many requests have been made. One other fact of Ireland's claim to the line of the Tribe of Judah is their flag. It consists of a white background with a red cross. On the upright of the cross is a crown, in the center of the cross is the Star of David, and in the center of the star is a red hand.

Flag of Northern Ireland

The crown represents the Scepter Line of Judah, the star represents the line of David (Perez), and the red hand represents Zarah the twin brother of Perez, sons of Judah.

The evidence seems sufficient of Jeremiah replanting the line of Perez in Ireland, and uniting it with the Zarah line. The documentation of this truth would fill volumes. However, the overall purpose of this book is to show that by God's Word and historical events God's promise to bring the Scepter Line into fulfillment through Judah and the Birthright line through Joseph and his two sons, Ephraim and Manasseh has been fulfilled. This further documents the groundwork, which has been laid and fulfilled through Great Britain and the United States, the Birthright blessings unconditionally promised.

Now, we can say, "the rest is history."

WHY THE BLINDNESS OF ISRAEL AND JUDAH?

Scripture identifies two great sins that caused both Israel and Judah to be blinded. They happened at different times, were different sins, and had different effects. The book of Exodus identifies why Israel (the 10 northern tribes) was blinded and lost its identity. In Exodus 13, God establishes his Passover to celebrate his deliverance of the Children of Israel out of Egypt. In verse nine he says, *9 And it shall be for a sign unto thee upon thine hand, and for a memorial between thine eyes, that the LORD'S law may be in thy mouth: for with a strong hand hath the LORD brought thee out of Egypt.* (Ex 13:9) In 12:24, God had already told the Israelites, *And ye shall observe this thing for an ordinance to thee and to thy sons for ever.* (Ex 12:24) and then in chapter 31 we read;

> 12 And the LORD spake unto Moses, saying, 13 Speak thou also unto the children of Israel, saying, Verily my sabbaths ye shall keep: for it *is a sign between me and you throughout your generations*; that *ye* may know that I *am* the LORD that doth sanctify you. 14 Ye shall keep the sabbath therefore; for it *is* holy unto you: every one that defileth it shall surely be put to death: for whosoever doeth *any* work therein, that soul shall be cut off from among his people. 15 Six days may work be done; but in the seventh *is* the sabbath of rest, holy to the LORD: whosoever doeth *any* work in the sabbath day, he shall surely be put to death. 16 Wherefore the children of Israel shall keep the sabbath, to observe the sabbath throughout their generations, *for* a perpetual covenant. 17 It *is* a sign between me and the children of Israel for ever: for *in* six days the LORD made heaven and earth, and on the seventh day he rested, and was refreshed. 18 And he gave unto Moses, when he had made an end of communing with him upon mount Sinai, two tables of testimony, tables of stone, written with the finger of God. Ex 31:12-18

Concerning the Sabbath, God says it is to be a perpetual covenant between himself and the Children of Israel. God emphasizes the fact that it is to be perpetual, observed by all generations, and last forever. This was God's will concerning the Sabbath signifying it as a sign of their relationship to him. A sign serves to help identify, distinguish, or set apart, one thing or a people from another thing or people.

Fast-forward to 1 Kings 12, some of which has been covered in an earlier chapter. Here, however, we want to especially notice what Jeroboam did as soon as he set up his kingdom in Samaria. Jeroboam was an Ephrathite who inherited the 10 Tribes, now called the Lost 10 Tribes.

> 25 Then Jeroboam built Shechem in mount Ephraim, and dwelt therein; and went out from thence, and built Penuel. 26 And Jeroboam said in his heart, Now shall the kingdom return to the house of David: 27 If this people go up to do sacrifice in the house of the LORD at Jerusalem, then shall the heart of this people turn again unto their Lord, *even* unto Rehoboam king of Judah, and they shall kill me, and go again to Rehoboam king of Judah. 28 Whereupon the king took counsel, and made two calves *of* gold, and said unto them, It is too much for you to go up to Jerusalem: behold thy gods, O Israel, which brought thee up out of the land of Egypt.
>
> 29 And he set the one in Bethel, and the other put he in Dan. 30 And this thing became a sin: for the people went *to worship* before the one, *even* unto Dan. 31 And he made an house of high places, and made priests of the lowest of the people, which were not of the sons of Levi. 32 And Jeroboam ordained a feast in the eighth month, on the fifteenth day of the month, like unto the feast that *is* in Judah, and he offered upon the altar. So did he in Bethel, sacrificing unto the calves that he had made: and he placed in Bethel the priests of the high places which he had made. 33 So he offered upon the altar which he had made in Bethel the fifteenth day of the eighth month, *even* in the month which he had devised of his own heart; and ordained a feast unto

the children of Israel: and he offered upon the altar, and burnt incense. 1 Kings 12:25-33

In this passage, we follow the plight of Jeroboam. Fearing for his kingdom and his life, he did not want his people to return to Jerusalem and worship the true God. To stop them he set up two golden calves, one in Dan and the other at Bethel. Proclaiming them the gods of the people; he installed the non-Levite Priests to lead in pagan worship. Perhaps the most damning act of Jeroboam, and one that seems to have made God simply say "enough," is recorded in verse 32. He changed both the day and the month of Sabbath and Passover observations. The very Commandments that God said would be a sign between him and his people forever. I call these test commandments; they were intended to test the faithfulness of the people. When Jeroboam and the people violated these tests, God would cast them out of his sight (2 Kings 17:18). In Hosea, he puts it this way, you are not my people, and I will not be your God (Hosea 1:9).

In their sin, they lost all contact with God. This resulted in a blinding of the people toward the true God. Because of this, they lost their identity and were scattered throughout the world. Result; to the unlearned in God's Word, they became the 10 Lost Tribes.

Judah's blindness came much later as a result of another national sin. The apostle John put it this way, *He came unto his own, and his own received him not.* (John 1:11) Judah was a willing participant in Israel's sentence but as a separate nation. Both had a different destiny. Judah was designated as the line from which the scepter (Christ) would come. Additionally, they were designated as the recipients of the law.

What advantage then hath the Jew? or what profit is there of circumcision? ² *Much every way: chiefly, because that unto them were committed the oracles of God.* (Romans 3:1-2) Of course, the oracles, or law, were given to all of Israel. Paul is referring to just the Jews, of whom he was one. He is explaining to the Romans that in Christ there is no difference.

However, the Nation of Judah's (Jews) greatest sin was rejecting the true Messiah when he came. This rejection was the final act that causes blindness to the Jews. They kept the law, after a fashion, and kept the Sabbath, but failed to see God's work through Christ. Even still, the goodness of God is in effect. He continues to watch over them and will bring them back to him. At that point, he will open their spiritual eyes and forgive the sins.

> [25] For I would not, brethren, that ye should be ignorant of this mystery, lest ye should be wise in your own conceits; that blindness in part is happened to Israel, until the fulness of the Gentiles be come in. [26] And so all Israel shall be saved: as it is written, There shall come out of Sion the Deliverer, and shall turn away ungodliness from Jacob: [27] For this *is* my covenant unto them, when I shall take away their sins. [28] As concerning the gospel, *they are* enemies for your sakes: but as touching the election, *they are* beloved for the fathers' sakes. [29] For the gifts and calling of God *are* without repentance. [30] For as ye in times past have not believed God, yet have now obtained mercy through their unbelief: [31] Even so have these also now not believed, that through your mercy they also may obtain mercy. [32] For God hath concluded them all in unbelief, that he might have mercy upon all. [33] O the depth of the riches both of the wisdom and knowledge of God! how unsearchable *are* his judgments, and his ways past finding out! Romans 11:25-33

In spite of all this, the Jewish nation can claim one blessing from God that no other nation or people on earth can claim. It is simple yet very profound; they all know who they are. For more than 4000 years, regardless of where they had been driven, scattered, or persecuted, they remained Jews. (See Psalms 137 and the book of Nehemiah)

Ask any Jew today who he is and where he would really like to be? He will likely tell you about his Jewish heritage and his desire to return to the homeland.

Why have the Jews retained this identity for all these centuries? Remember the test commandments that was the sign between God and his people? It was forever to be an identifying mark, which would distinguish them from all others. They keep the Sabbath in their own way, proclaim his laws and honor his feast days. They keep their identity as Jews, even though blinded for their sin of unbelief in Christ's identity.

Israel, the birthright nation, did not keep this test commandment. As a result, they lost their identity, their language, and were scattered throughout the world.

So say the Scriptures.

ENGLAND'S CORONATION CHAIR

History tells us that the coronation stone was brought to England from Ireland. There is substantial historical evidence that in 583A.D Jeremiah brought the stone to Ireland from Judah. In 1296A.D, King Edward I. constructed the Coronation Chair to celebrate his own crowning. The base of this chair rests upon a stone. This coronation chair or thrown has been in constant use since that time. An earlier use of the stone for a coronation was when Eochaide the Herman was crowned King of Ireland. This event took place when he married Tea Tephi, the daughter of Zedekiah, king of Judah. This wedding took place after Zedekiah was conquered by Nebuchadnezzar in 586 B.C. and Jeremiah took Tea Tephi to Ireland.

Earlier, all the Kings of Israel, and later the Kings of Judah were crowned either on or beside the stone. (Remember that Scepter shall not depart from Judah - Genesis 49:10) Further confirmation of the use of the stone pillar is found in 2 King's 11:14.

The marriage of Eochaide, the King of Ireland, and one of Zedekiah's daughters (Tea Tephi, a princess of Judah) completed the fulfillment of Jacob's command that Judah should rule over the 12 Tribes. Eochaid descended from the Zarah Line of Judah and Tea Tephi was of the Perez Line of Judah. The Zarah Line, as the firstborn, ruled the 12 Tribes in Egypt following the death of Jacob. With the arrival of Tea Tephi in Ireland and her later marriage to the Milesian King Eochaid, the Lines of Zarah and Perez (twin sons of Judah) were united. This event healed the breach dividing the two Lines. From this marriage union, all the future kings and queens of Northwest Europe would descend.

In Ezekiel 21: 25-27, God promises,

[25] And thou, profane wicked prince of Israel, whose day is come, when iniquity shall have an end, [26] Thus saith the Lord GOD; Remove the diadem, and take off the crown: this shall not be the same: exalt him that is low, and abase him that is high. [27] I will overturn, overturn, overturn, it: and it shall be no more, until he come whose right it is; and I will give it him.

WHAT ABOUT THE CHURCH?

¹⁷ Think not that I am come to destroy the law, or the prophets: I am not come to destroy, but to fulfil.   Matt 5:17

Christ, the head of the church, the chief cornerstone, the one with whom we will reign in the millennial kingdom says; he came to fulfill the law and the prophets. To fulfill something means one must meet the requirements of that object.[22] What does a prophet do? He makes prophecies. We have just seen a number of the prophecies regarding the re-gathering of Israel and Judah. Now, let us consider how this fits into the calling out of the Body of Christ, the Church. There is absolutely no conflict in these two great truths, rather they compliment and confirm one another.

> [11] Wherefore remember, that ye being in time past Gentiles in the flesh, who are called Uncircumcision by that which is called the Circumcision in the flesh made by hands; [12] That at that time ye were without Christ, being aliens from the commonwealth of Israel, and strangers from the covenants of promise, having no hope, and without God in the world: [13] But now in Christ Jesus ye who sometimes were far off are made nigh by the blood of Christ.
>
> [14] For he is our peace, who hath made both one, and hath broken down the middle wall of partition between us; [15] Having abolished in his flesh the enmity, even the law of commandments contained in ordinances; for to make in himself of twain one new man, so making peace; [16] And that he might reconcile both unto God in one body by the cross, having slain the enmity thereby: [17] And came and preached

---

[22] Fulfill: to put into effect: EXECUTE b : to meet the requirements of – Merriam-Webster's 11th Collegiate Edition, 2003

peace to you which were afar off, and to them that were nigh. [18] For through him we both have access by one Spirit unto the Father. [19] Now therefore ye are no more strangers and foreigners, but fellowcitizens with the saints, and of the household of God; [20] And are built upon the foundation of the apostles and prophets, Jesus Christ himself being the chief corner stone; [21] In whom all the building fitly framed together groweth unto an holy temple in the Lord: [22] In whom ye also are builded together for an habitation of God through the Spirit. Eph 2:11-22

These verses speak of several conditions of the Gentile Church throughout they Church Age.

- In time past they were Gentiles - 11
- They were without Christ - 12
- They were aliens from the Commonwealth of Israel - 12
- They were strangers from the covenants of promise - 12
- They had no hope without God - 13
- Now in Christ, they were made nigh to the blood of Christ - 13 Christ is our peace, and has broken down the wall a partition between the church and Israel - 14
- They had been reconciled unto God by the cross - 16
- Through Christ we have access to the Father by his Spirit - 18
- The Gentiles are no longer strangers, or foreigners, but fellow-citizens with the saints in the house-hold of God - 19
- They, the church, are built upon the foundations of the apostles and prophets with Jesus as the cornerstone - 20
- All, meaning both Israel and the Church, fit together in a Holy Temple of the Lord -21
- The temple where both Israel and the Church now

abide is the habitation of God through the Spirit

These verses, so rich in truth, leaving no reason to misunderstand. There is much more that identifies just who is being brought into what. Please note that nothing is said about the Jews. This is about the Commonwealth of Israel, including those we would label the Jews, the Church, and for our purposes here especially the supposedly Ten Lost Tribes, often innocently referred to as Gentiles.

[21] But to Israel he saith, All day long I have stretched forth my hands unto a disobedient and gainsaying people. [1] I say then, Hath God cast away his people? God forbid. For I also am an Israelite, of the seed of Abraham, *of* the tribe of Benjamin. [2] God hath not cast away his people which he foreknew. Wot ye not what the scripture saith of Elias? how he maketh intercession to God against Israel, saying,

[3] Lord, they have killed thy prophets, and digged down thine altars; and I am left alone, and they seek my life.

[4] But what saith the answer of God unto him? I have reserved to myself seven thousand men, who have not bowed the knee to *the image of* Baal.

[5] Even so then at this present time also there is a remnant according to the election of grace. [6] And if by grace, then *is it* no more of works: otherwise grace is no more grace. But if *it be* of works, then is it no more grace: otherwise work is no more work. [7] What then? Israel hath not obtained that which he seeketh for; but the election hath obtained it, and the rest were blinded [8] (According as it is written, God hath given them the spirit of slumber, eyes that they should not see, and ears that they should not hear;) unto this day. [9] And David saith, Let their table be made a snare, and a trap, and a stumblingblock, and a recompence unto them: [10] Let their eyes be darkened, that they may not see, and bow down their back alway. [11] I say then, Have they stumbled that they should fall? God forbid: but *rather* through their fall salvation *is come* unto the Gentiles, for to provoke them to jealousy. [12] Now if the fall of them *be* the riches of the world,

and the diminishing of them the riches of the Gentiles; how much more their fulness? ¹³ For I speak to you Gentiles, inasmuch as I am the apostle of the Gentiles, I magnify mine office: ¹⁴ If by any means I may provoke to emulation *them which are* my flesh, and might save some of them.

¹⁵ For if the casting away of them *be* the reconciling of the world, what *shall* the receiving *of them be*, but life from the dead?

¹⁶ For if the firstfruit *be* holy, the lump *is* also *holy:* and if the root *be* holy, so *are* the branches. ¹⁷ And if some of the branches be broken off, and thou, being a wild olive tree, wert grafted in among them, and with them partakest of the root and fatness of the olive tree; ¹⁸ Boast not against the branches. But if thou boast, thou bearest not the root, but the root thee. ¹⁹ Thou wilt say then, The branches were broken off, that I might be grafted in. ²⁰ Well; because of unbelief they were broken off, and thou standest by faith. Be not highminded, but fear: ²¹ For if God spared not the natural branches, *take heed* lest he also spare not thee. ²² Behold therefore the goodness and severity of God: on them which fell, severity; but toward thee, goodness, if thou continue in *his* goodness: otherwise thou also shalt be cut off. ²³ And they also, if they abide not still in unbelief, shall be grafted in: for God is able to graft them in again. ²⁴ For if thou wert cut out of the olive tree which is wild by nature, and wert grafted contrary to nature into a good olive tree: how much more shall these, which be the natural *branches*, be grafted into their own olive tree? ²⁵ For I would not, brethren, that ye should be ignorant of this mystery, lest ye should be wise in your own conceits; that blindness in part is happened to Israel, until the fulness of the Gentiles be come in.

²⁶ And so all Israel shall be saved: as it is written, There shall come out of Sion the Deliverer, and shall turn away ungodliness from Jacob:

²⁷ For this *is* my covenant unto them, when I shall take away their sins. Romans 10:21 - 11:27

Paul, writing to the church at Rome, is dealing with many misunderstandings of the early church. Many Jews had come into the church and could not understand why salvation was offered to anyone else. In Romans, and other letters, Paul dealt with the "great mystery" that God would even offer salvation to a non-Jew. Here, he assures both Jew and Gentile that God had not forgotten "all Israel" which included both the scepter and birthright lines. Each is included in God's grace and New Covenant. Most importantly, he was reminding the Gentiles that they were the wild olive branch that had been grafted into the root of Israel. Furthermore, God had not cast away his people (11:1), of which a remnant remained according to the election of grace. By his grace his covenant remains, their sins will be taken away, and he would call them back.

Paul also mentions of a period of blindness for Israel. An important aspect of understanding God's working is to see that this blindness is temporary and God will one day end it.

WHAT ABOUT NOW?

God has now fulfilled his unconditional promise to Abraham, Isaac, and Jacob. Thru the linage of Juda, Christ has come offering salvation to all. Thru the linage of Joseph, (Ephraim and Manasseh) he has brought untold material wealth and prosperity to "a company of nations" and a "great nation." Thru this wealth and prosperity, all of the nations of the earth have shared in God's goodness.

But what about now? God has now been relegated to a low priority at best and to total insignificance and non-existence in so many millions of people. Human secularism and self-indulgence has swept the world including the British Empire and America. Great Britain is no longer "great", having lost eighty-percent of its holdings. What remains of the Commonwealth has turned away from God to a great extent. In our beloved United States, we proclaim "God Bless America", while endorsing ungodliness never before thought of by our founding fathers. Abortion is one of our national sins. The acceptance of homosexuality and so-called "gay marriage" is putrid in the nostrils of God. He will not overlook this decadence. The judgments of nations is just as much a truth of God's Word as is the judgment of the individual's own heart.

We see Egypt in the Exodus being judged and Babylon in Revelation also being judged. Most importantly, we see God's chosen people, including the Church judged and punished throughout his word. Specifically we read in Lev. 26 (previously quoted), the withholding of his blessings for over 2500 years because of sin. We also see the final warning of God's judgment. If, after he has kept his promise to the birthright nations, they turn from his word, God says:

²⁷ *And if ye will not for*²³ *all this hearken unto me, but walk contrary unto me;* **²⁸** *Then I will walk contrary unto you also in fury; and I, even I, will chastise you seven times for your sins.* (Lev 26:27-28 (KJV)) In God's series of warnings in this chapter, and in the light of other scriptures, it is consistent to apply the warning to the Last Days. It corresponds to the seven last plaques as described in The Revelation of John. If "Not for all this," referring to God's warnings and punishment, his people turn from God as this nation has done, then national judgment comes.

Other prophetic warnings clearly speak to Israel, wherever they are geographically, and Judah jointly in the Last Days. Amos states that God revealed <u>all</u> his plans, especially events of the Last Days, when he says: *7 Surely the Lord GOD will do nothing, but he revealeth his secret unto his servants the prophets.* (Amos 3:7 (KJV)) Jeremiah gives us a very clear illustration in chapter 30:1-9.

> ¹ The word that came to Jeremiah from the LORD, saying,
> ² Thus speaketh the LORD God of Israel, saying, Write thee all the words that I have spoken unto thee in a book. ³ For, lo, the days come, saith the LORD, that I will bring again the captivity of my people Israel and Judah, saith the LORD: and I will cause them to return to the land that I gave to their fathers, and they shall possess it. ⁴ And these are the words that the LORD spake concerning Israel and concerning Judah.
>
> ⁵ For thus saith the LORD; We have heard a voice of trembling, of fear, and not of peace. ⁶ Ask ye now, and see whether a man doth travail with child? wherefore do I see every man with his hands on his loins, as a woman in travail, and all faces are turned into paleness?
>
> ⁷ Alas! for that day is great, so that none is like it: it is even the time of Jacob's trouble; but he shall be saved out of

---

²³ "For" is also translated "after." Thus reading, "if ye will not after all this"

it. [8] For it shall come to pass in that day, saith the LORD of hosts, that I will break his yoke from off thy neck, and will burst thy bonds, and strangers shall no more serve themselves of him: [9] But they shall serve the LORD their God, and David their king, whom I will raise up unto them.

[10] Therefore fear thou not, O my servant Jacob, saith the LORD; neither be dismayed, O Israel: for, lo, I will save thee from afar, and thy seed from the land of their captivity; and Jacob shall return, and shall be in rest, and be quiet, and none shall make him afraid. [11] For I am with thee, saith the LORD, to save thee: though I make a full end of all nations whither I have scattered thee, yet will I not make a full end of thee: but I will correct thee in measure, and will not leave thee altogether unpunished. Jer 30:1-11 (KJV)

Here, Jeremiah identifies exactly to whom he is speaking and the time in which these events are to take place. In verse 4, God addresses both Israel and Judah. Israel, as a nation, ceased to exist some 130 years before the time of Jeremiah's writing. Judah, at this time, was in Babylonian captivity. God clearly proclaims in this prophecy that both will return to the land given their fathers, Palestine.

The passages above refer to two events that parallel other confirming scriptures.

- A day of travail and nothing like it ever before
- A time of Jacob's (not Judah) trouble
- This will cause both nations to turn to God, Israel and Judah with David (Christ) as King

Additionally in Jeremiah:

[15] For thus saith the LORD God of Israel unto me; Take the wine cup of this fury at my hand, and cause all the nations, to whom I send thee, to drink it. [16] And they shall drink, and be moved, and be mad, because of the sword that I will send among them. Jer 25:15-16 (KJV)

30 Therefore prophesy thou against them all these words, and say unto them, The LORD shall roar from on high, and utter his voice from his holy habitation; he shall mightily roar upon his habitation; he shall give a shout, as they that tread the grapes, against all the inhabitants of the earth.

31 A noise shall come even to the ends of the earth; for the LORD hath a controversy with the nations, he will plead with all flesh; he will give them that are wicked to the sword, saith the LORD.

32 Thus saith the LORD of hosts, Behold, evil shall go forth from nation to nation, and a great whirlwind shall be raised up from the coasts of the earth. **33** And the slain of the LORD shall be at that day from one end of the earth even unto the other end of the earth: they shall not be lamented, neither gathered, nor buried; they shall be dung upon the ground. **34** Howl, ye shepherds, and cry; and wallow yourselves in the ashes, ye principal of the flock: for the days of your slaughter and of your dispersions are accomplished; and ye shall fall like a pleasant vessel. **35** And the shepherds shall have no way to flee, nor the principal of the flock to escape. **36** A voice of the cry of the shepherds, and an howling of the principal of the flock, shall be heard: for the LORD hath spoiled their pasture. **37** And the peaceable habitations are cut down because of the fierce anger of the LORD. **38** He hath forsaken his covert, as the lion: for their land is desolate because of the fierceness of the oppressor, and because of his fierce anger. Jer 25:30-38 (KJV)

Notice that Revelation 14:17-20 uses similar wording as found in Jeremiah 25:15.

14 And I looked, and behold a white cloud, and upon the cloud *one* sat like unto the Son of man, having on his head a golden crown, and in his hand a sharp sickle. **15** And another angel came out of the temple, crying with a loud voice to him that sat on the cloud, Thrust in thy sickle, and reap: for the time is come for thee to reap; for the harvest of the earth is ripe. **16** And he that sat on the cloud thrust in his sickle on the earth; and the earth was reaped. **17** And another angel came out of the temple which is in heaven, he also having a sharp sickle.

18 And another angel came out from the altar, which had power over fire; and cried with a loud cry to him that had the sharp sickle, saying, Thrust in thy sharp sickle, and gather the clusters of the vine of the earth; for her grapes are fully ripe. **19** And the angel thrust in his sickle into the earth, and gathered the vine of the earth, and cast *it* into the great winepress of the wrath of God. **20** And the winepress was trodden without the city, and blood came out of the winepress, even unto the horse bridles, by the space of a thousand *and* six hundred furlongs. Rev 14:14-20 (KJV)

This prophecy does not focus on the immediate future for Israel/Juda, but is addressed to the end of the earth, "Nation to nation...from the coast of the earth." Verse 33 continues the same theme, "from one end of the earth even to the other end". Verse 34-36 addresses the shepherds; the religious leaders who have failed to guide the flock.

It might come as a surprise to some who profess themselves as New Testament Churches to discover that the Old Testament was not written for the "Jews" only. In conflict with this notion is the book of Joel for example, which deals mostly with end-time prophecies. More specifically, it deals with a future time of God re-gathering Judah and Israel under David (Christ) as king.

15 Alas for the day! for the day of the LORD is at hand, and as a destruction from the Almighty shall it come. **16** Is not the meat cut off before our eyes, yea, joy and gladness from the house of our God? **17** The seed is rotten under their clods, the garners are laid desolate, the barns are broken down; for the corn is withered. **18** How do the beasts groan! the herds of cattle are perplexed, because they have no pasture; yea, the flocks of sheep are made desolate.

19 O LORD, to thee will I cry: for the fire hath devoured the pastures of the wilderness, and the flame hath burned all the trees of the field.

20 The beasts of the field cry also unto thee: for the rivers of waters are dried up, and the fire hath devoured the pastures of the wilderness. Joel 1:15-20 (KJV)   **1** Blow ye the trumpet in Zion, and sound an alarm in my holy mountain: let all the inhabitants of the land tremble: for the day of the LORD cometh, for it is nigh at hand; **2** A day of darkness and of gloominess, a day of clouds and of thick darkness, as the morning spread upon the mountains: a great people and a strong; there hath not been ever the like, neither shall be any more after it, even to the years of many generations. Joel 2:1-2 (KJV)

At this point, it is beneficial to look at what Paul wrote to the Romans in chapter 11 regarding the church and Israel. Focus especially on verses 1, 5, 13, and 16 – 25.

1 I say then, Hath God cast away his people? God forbid. For I also am an Israelite, of the seed of Abraham, of the tribe of Benjamin.

2 God hath not cast away his people which he foreknew. Wot ye not what the scripture saith of Elias? how he maketh intercession to God against Israel, saying, **3** Lord, they have killed thy prophets, and digged down thine altars; and I am left alone, and they seek my life

4 But what saith the answer of God unto him? I have reserved to myself seven thousand men, who have not bowed the knee to the image of Baal. **5** Even so then at this present time also there is a remnant according to the election of grace. **6** And if by grace, then is it no more of works: otherwise grace is no more grace. But if it be of works, then is it no more grace: otherwise work is no more work. **7** What then? Israel hath not obtained that which he seeketh for; but the election hath obtained it, and the rest were blinded **8** (According as it is written, God hath given them the spirit of slumber, eyes that they should not see, and ears that they should not hear;) unto this day. **9** And David saith, Let their table be made a snare, and a trap, and a stumblingblock, and a recompence unto them: **10** Let their eyes be darkened, that they may not see, and bow down their back alway. **11** I say then, Have they stumbled that they should fall? God forbid: but rather through their fall salvation is come unto the Gentiles, for to provoke them to jealousy. ¹² Now if the fall of them be the riches of the world, and the diminishing of them the riches of the Gentiles; how much more their fulness? ¹³ For I speak to you Gentiles, inasmuch as I am the apostle of the Gentiles, I magnify mine office: ¹⁴ If by any means I may provoke to emulation them which are my flesh, and might save some of them. ¹⁵ For if the casting away of them be the reconciling of the world, what shall the receiving of them be, but life from the dead? ¹⁶ For if the firstfruit be holy, the lump is also holy: and if the root be holy, so are the branches. ¹⁷ And if some of the branches be broken off, and thou, being a wild olive tree, wert grafted in among them, and with them partakest of the root and fatness of the olive tree; ¹⁸ Boast not against the branches. But if thou boast, thou bearest not the root, but the root thee. ¹⁹ Thou wilt say then, The branches were broken off, that I might be grafted in. ²⁰ Well; because of unbelief they were broken off, and thou standest by faith. Be not highminded, but fear: ²¹ For if God spared not the natural branches, take heed lest he also spare not thee.

²² Behold therefore the goodness and severity of God: on them which fell, severity; but toward thee, goodness, if thou continue in his goodness: otherwise thou also shalt be cut off. ²³ And they also, if they abide not still in unbelief, shall be grafted in: for God is able to graft them in again. ²⁴ For if thou wert cut out of the olive tree which is wild by nature, and wert grafted contrary to nature into a good olive tree: how much more shall these, which be the natural branches, be grafted into their own olive tree?

²⁵ For I would not, brethren, that ye should be ignorant of this mystery, lest ye should be wise in your own conceits; that blindness in part is happened to Israel, until the fulness of the Gentiles be come in.

²⁶ And so all Israel shall be saved: as it is written, There shall come out of Sion the Deliverer, and shall turn away ungodliness from Jacob: ²⁷ For this is my covenant unto them, when I shall take away their sins. ²⁸ As concerning the gospel, they are enemies for your sakes: but as touching the election, they are beloved for the fathers' sakes. ²⁹ For the gifts and calling of God are without repentance. ³⁰ For as ye in times past have not believed God, yet have now obtained mercy through their unbelief: ³¹ Even so have

these also now not believed, that through your mercy they also may obtain mercy. ³² For God hath concluded them all in unbelief, that he might have mercy upon all.

³³ O the depth of the riches both of the wisdom and knowledge of God! how unsearchable are his judgments, and his ways past finding out!

³⁴ For who hath known the mind of the Lord? or who hath been his counsellor? ³⁵ Or who hath first given to him, and it shall be recompensed unto him again? ³⁶ For of him, and through him, and to him, are all things: to whom be glory for ever. Amen. Romans 11:1-36 (KJV)

Paul uses the visual illustration of branches of a grape vine. Those that do not produce are replaced, but the whole vine is not discarded.

- God has not cast away his people Israel – vs. 1
- There is still a remnant of Israel – vs. 5
- He is speaking to the gentile church at Rome – vs. 13
- Israel is the true root and the church is the wild olive branch grafted in – vs. 16 - 25

Paul addresses this same issue of the rightful place of Israel in conjunction to the church in Ephesians. Remember that the church of Ephesus is spoken of quite well in the book of Revelation.

¹¹ Wherefore remember, that ye being in time past Gentiles in the flesh, who are called Uncircumcision by that which is called the Circumcision in the flesh made by hands; ¹² That at that time ye were without Christ, being aliens from the commonwealth of Israel, and strangers from the covenants of promise, having no hope, and without God in the world: ¹³ But now in Christ Jesus ye who sometimes were far off are made nigh by the blood of Christ.

¹⁴ For he is our peace, who hath made both one, and hath broken down the middle wall of partition between us;

¹⁵ Having abolished in his flesh the enmity, even the law of commandments contained in ordinances; for to make in himself of twain one new man, so making peace; ¹⁶ And that he might reconcile both unto God in one body by the cross, having slain the enmity thereby:

¹⁷ And came and preached peace to you which were afar off, and to them that were nigh. ¹⁸ For through him we both have access by one Spirit unto the Father. ¹⁹ Now therefore ye are no more strangers and foreigners, but fellowcitizens with the saints, and of the household of God; ²⁰ And are built upon the foundation of the apostles and prophets, Jesus Christ himself being the chief corner stone; ²¹ In whom all the building fitly framed together groweth unto an holy temple in the Lord: ²² In whom ye also are builded together for an habitation of God through the Spirit.   Eph 2:11-22 (KJV)

Paul makes several key points in this passage concerning the glorious church.

- They were without Christ in the past – vs. 12
- They were aliens from the commonwealth of Israel – vs. 12
- Strangers from the covenant and possessed no hope without God – vs. 12
- Now through the blood of Christ they are now in the commonwealth - vs. 13
- No longer strangers or aliens they stand as fellow Citizens of Israel – vs. 19
- The church is built upon the foundation of both the apostles and the prophets - vs. 20

The message of the apostles spotlighted the gospel of Jesus. His sacrifice on the cross opened the door to the Kingdom of God for all to receive through God's grace. Christ made this possible by tearing down the spiritual walls separating the gentiles from God's Kingdom.

Micah – the God, the Bad, and the Ugly

In Micah 4:1-7, we find the good in the Last Days.

> [1] But in the Last Days it shall come to pass, that the mountain of the house of the LORD shall be established in the top of the mountains, and it shall be exalted above the hills; and people shall flow unto it.
>
> [2] And many nations shall come, and say, Come, and let us go up to the mountain of the LORD, and to the house of the God of Jacob; and he will teach us of his ways, and we will walk in his paths: for the law shall go forth of Zion, and the word of the LORD from Jerusalem.
>
> [3] And he shall judge among many people, and rebuke strong nations afar off; and they shall beat their swords into plowshares, and their spears into pruninghooks: nation shall not lift up a sword against nation, neither shall they learn war any more. [4] But they shall sit every man under his vine and under his fig tree; and none shall make them afraid: for the mouth of the LORD of hosts hath spoken it. [5] For all people will walk every one in the name of his god, and we will walk in the name of the LORD our God for ever and ever. [6] In that day, saith the LORD, will I assemble her that halteth, and I will gather her that is driven out, and her that I have afflicted; [7] And I will make her that halted a remnant, and her that was cast far off a strong nation: and the LORD shall reign over them in mount Zion from henceforth, even for ever.   Micah 4:1-7 (KJV)

Micah 5:7 – 15 depicts both the Good and the Bad in the same Last Days.

> [7] And the remnant of Jacob shall be in the midst of many people as a dew from the LORD, as the showers upon the grass, that tarrieth not for man, nor waiteth for the sons of men. [8] And the remnant of Jacob shall be among the Gentiles in the midst of many people as a lion among the beasts of the forest, as a young lion among the flocks of sheep: who, if he go through, both treadeth down, and teareth in pieces, and none can deliver. [9] Thine hand shall be lifted up upon

thine adversaries, and all thine enemies shall be cut off. ¹⁰ And it shall come to pass in that day, saith the LORD, that I will cut off thy horses out of the midst of thee, and I will destroy thy chariots: ¹¹ And I will cut off the cities of thy land, and throw down all thy strong holds: ¹² And I will cut off witchcrafts out of thine hand; and thou shalt have no more soothsayers: ¹³ Thy graven images also will I cut off, and thy standing images out of the midst of thee; and thou shalt no more worship the work of thine hands. ¹⁴ And I will pluck up thy groves out of the midst of thee: so will I destroy thy cities. ¹⁵ And I will execute vengeance in anger and fury upon the heathen, such as they have not heard.   Micah 5:7-15 (KJV)

Even as the Last Days approach, God offers a measure of Hope to the ugly.

¹⁶ The nations shall see and be confounded at all their might: they shall lay their hand upon their mouth, their ears shall be deaf. ¹⁷ They shall lick the dust like a serpent, they shall move out of their holes like worms of the earth: they shall be afraid of the LORD our God, and shall fear because of thee.   Micah 7:16-17 (KJV)

The focal point of each of these Micah passages is the Last Days.   Micah is not warning Israel or Judah about the days of their immediate future.   Micah 5:7 paints a wonderful picture of Jacob (Israel) "as the dew of the Lord." They are like "showers upon the grass."   In Deuteronomy God spoke Through Moses directly to Joseph and the birthright children wherever they may be in the world. The word pictures used in Deuteronomy 33:13 – 16 are very similar to those of Micah 5:7.

¹³ And of Joseph he said, Blessed of the LORD be his land, for the precious things of heaven, for the dew, and for the deep that coucheth beneath, ¹⁴ And for the precious fruits brought forth by the sun, and for the precious things put forth by the moon,

¹⁵ And for the chief things of the ancient mountains, and for the precious things of the lasting hills, ¹⁶ And for the precious things of the earth and fulness thereof, and for the good will of him that dwelt in the bush: let the blessing come upon the head of Joseph, and upon the top of the head of him that was separated from his brethren.   Deut 33:13-16 (KJV)

The final verses of Micah again address those of the blessed remnant.

¹⁸ Who is a God like unto thee, that pardoneth iniquity, and passeth by the transgression of the remnant of his heritage? he retaineth not his anger for ever, because he delighteth in mercy. ¹⁹ He will turn again, he will have compassion upon us; he will subdue our iniquities; and thou wilt cast all their sins into the depths of the sea. ²⁰ Thou wilt perform the truth to Jacob, and the mercy to Abraham, which thou hast sworn unto our fathers from the days of old.   Micah 7:18-20 (KJV)

This "blessed remnant" displays the ultimate extent of God's mercy and grace. It confirms the promise he made to Abraham in Genesis 22 as unconditional even thou hundreds of years would pass while the blessings are withheld. The sin, which caused God to withhold the blessings, would not be forever. In the end, the righteous, made so by the grace of God through Christ, will be saved.

---

²⁴ ⁴ And I heard the number of them which were sealed: *and there were* sealed an hundred *and* forty *and* four thousand of all the tribes of the children of Israel. ···.
⁹ After this I beheld, and, lo, a great multitude, which no man could number, of all nations, and kindreds, and people, and tongues, stood before the throne, and before the Lamb, clothed with white robes, and palms in their hands; Rev 7:4-9 (KJV)

The "remnant" of God are spoken of in many places in the New Testament. Both Paul in Romans and John in Revelation speak of a "remnant" of God's people. These are not different groups of people; it is the same remnant in each instance. In Revelation 7, the servants of God are sealed, a total of one-hundred and forty-four thousand. The sealed are not just anybody, they are of the tribes of Israel. They are separate from the multitude of the nations also depicted in Revelation 7.[24] The glorious truth that is confirmed in the mouth of two witnesses (or more) is found in Revelation 7:9. Through the words of the praise of the multitude (witnesses), scripture confirms itself as truth. John 7:39 and 2 Tim. 2:15 implore us to "search the scripture" and "rightly divide the word of truth".

The prophet Isaiah, in 28:9-10, also gave instruction of the importance of understanding God's Word.

> [9] Whom shall he teach knowledge? and whom shall he make to understand doctrine? them that are weaned from the milk, and drawn from the breasts. [10] For precept must be upon precept, precept upon precept; line upon line, line upon line; here a little, and there a little: Isaiah 28:9-10 (KJV

We are told in these scriptures to:

- Be weaned from the breast
- Search the scriptures
- Rightly Divide the scriptures
- Understand knowledge and teach knowledge by taking line upon line precept (truth) upon truth

In Hebrews 5, the writer is speaking of the teachings of Christ when he says much of the same thing.

> [11] Of whom we have many things to say, and hard to be uttered, seeing ye are dull of hearing. [12] For when for the time ye ought to be teachers, ye have need that one teach you again which be the first principles of the oracles of God; and are become such as have need of milk, and not of strong meat.
>
> [13] For every one that useth milk is unskilful in the word of righteousness: for he is a babe. [14] But strong meat belongeth to them that are of full age, even those who by reason of use have their senses exercised to discern both good and evil. Heb 5:11-14 (KJV)

In the mouth of two witnesses, and in the case of Bible prophecy more than two prophets, truths are established. So much for the doubters and critics who will say that this writer is just using "scattered" verses to try to prove a point. What a great compliment to the truths of God's Word. That is exactly how you gain knowledge, by using God's Words and not our own.

What an indictment on the carnal, lukewarm church of these Last Days and for their feel good messages proclaimed. Little is proclaimed about who we are and what God really has in store for the true over-comers. Nothing taught about ruling and reigning with Christ here on this earth.

This book is not about discovering "new" truths. Such an incorrect conclusion undermines the entire purpose of the book. It is about assembling Biblical truths and historical events that have been in place, some for over five thousand years

All the Kings Horses

Bible prophecy continues in Hosea and Rev. 7 regarding the nation's fate of many nations in the Last Days.

⁵ And the pride of Israel doth testify to his face: therefore shall Israel and Ephraim fall in their iniquity; Judah also shall fall with them. ⁶ They shall go with their flocks and with their herds to seek the LORD; but they shall not find him; he hath withdrawn himself from them. ⁷ They have dealt treacherously against the LORD: for they have begotten strange children: now shall a moth devour them with their portions.

⁸ Blow ye the cornet in Gibeah, and the trumpet in Ramah: cry aloud at Bethaven, after thee, O Benjamin. ⁹ Ephraim shall be desolate in the day of rebuke: among the tribes of Israel have I made known that which shall surely be. Hosea 5:5-9 (KJV)

What About Now (continued)

Here is the specific naming of Israel and Ephraim (America and Britain) along with Juda, now the land (country) of Israel. The clear message of the text is that we will fall in our own inequity.

⁴ Ah sinful nation, a people laden with iniquity, a seed of evildoers, children that are corrupters: they have forsaken the LORD, they have provoked the Holy One of Israel unto anger, they are gone away backwards. Isaiah 1:4 (KJV)

Yes, God is angry with America. He is angry with us for killing millions of our most innocent and helpless calling it a "convenient procedure." He is angry that we are grinding out movies and television programs that show incest, bestiality, homosexuality, child rape and all types of ungodliness calling it "art." We teach even school children wickedness in every imaginable way while denying them access to the Word of God. It is impossible to list and keep up with the pace of new national sins and corrupt acts of this once God fearing nation. We truly have "gone away backward." The prayer of this writer is for this nation to follow the instructions of 2 Chron. 7:14[26] before it is too late. Let this call from God wake up America, wake up the church, and wake up the people of God.

Good News at Last!

[26] **14** If my people, which are called by my name, shall humble themselves, and pray, and seek my face, and turn from their wicked ways; then will I hear from heaven, and will forgive their sin, and will heal their land. 2 Chron 7:14 (KJV)

> For these be the days of vengeance, that all things which are written may be fulfilled. (Luke 21:22 (KJV)) And when these things begin to come to pass, then look up, and lift up your heads; for your redemption draweth nigh. Luke 21:28 (KJV)

"Surely I come quickly." Amen!

Even so, come, Lord Jesus

God Blessed America
No More

Also Available
➢ Discussion Starter
➢ Teaching Guide
➢ Student Study Guide/Workbook

Take this incredible study to your:
- Book Club/Discussion Group
- Small Group Study
- Church Discipleship Group
- Sunday Morning/Sunday Night Study Class
- Wherever there is an interest in understanding Biblical Prophecy in today's world

The author is making available these teaching/study materials so you can use this book with any size group. They are perfect to help you guide your group/class to begin looking at how America gained God's favor - and how it is in danger of seeing those blessings removed from our beloved country.

It is the responsibility of every generation to read the "signs of the times," with the understanding that these are the Last Days. Each current event and passing day requires that we re-examine our world <u>through the eyes of Scripture</u>; not because Scripture has changed, but because we can have new insight as prophecy is fulfilled.

Dr. William Class

**THIS MATERIAL AVAILABLE ONLY FROM
MANESSEH PUBLISHERS**
at www.info@artofthestates.com
DISCOVER or **VISA** contact us at
1-800-771-3246
Special discounts available for churches, prayer groups, and other church-related groups

Please have credit card No. ready when calling

Printed in the United States
98135LV00005B/181-222/A